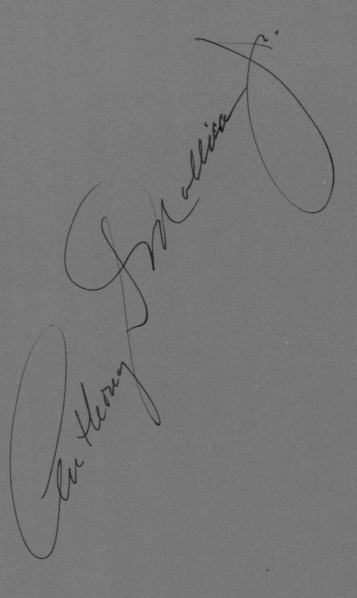

CLASSIC BOATS *of the* THOUSAND ISLANDS

CLASSIC BOATS *of the* THOUSAND ISLANDS

ANTHONY MOLLICA JR. & GEORGE FISCHER

The BOSTON
MILLS PRESS

In memory of John H. Wells,
humanitarian, historian, craftsman, teacher and friend, who realized the importance and
encouraged the collecting of stories and photographs of the wonderful vintage boats of the Thousand Islands.

A BOSTON MILLS PRESS BOOK

Copyright © 2005 Anthony S. Mollica and George Fischer

Published by Boston Mills Press, 2005
132 Main Street, Erin, Ontario N0B 1T0
Tel: 519-833-2407 Fax: 519-833-2195
e-mail: books@bostonmillspress.com
www.bostonmillspress.com

In Canada:
Distributed by Firefly Books Ltd.
66 Leek Crescent
Richmond Hill, Ontario, Canada L4B 1H1

In the United States:
Distributed by Firefly Books (U.S.) Inc.
P.O. Box 1338, Ellicott Station
Buffalo, New York 14205

The publisher acknowledges for their financial support of our publishing program,
the Canada Council, the Ontario Arts Council and the Government of Canada
through the Book Publishing Industry Development Program (BPIDP).

Photos of *North Star* on pages 132 and 133 courtesy of Denny Murdock.

Design by Gillian Stead

Printed in China

Publisher Cataloging-in-Publication Data   (U.S.)

Mollica, Anthony, 1932- .

Classic boats of the Thousand Islands /
Anthony Mollica Jr. ; photography by George Fischer. 1st ed.

[160] p. :   col. photos. ;   cm.

Includes bibliographical references and index.

Summary: A photographic and historic record of the Thousand Islands region's rich boatbuilding
heritage, including the development of the unique St. Lawrence skiff, its lavish custom runabouts
and sport boats, cruisers and yachts, and a tour of the Antique Boat Museum's in-water fleet and
the area's best boatbuilding and restoration shops.

ISBN 1-55046-441-8

1. Boatbuilding -- Thousand Islands (N.Y. and Ont.) -- History. 2. Boatyards -- Thousand Islands
(N.Y. and Ont.) -- History.   I. Fischer, George, 1954- .   II. Title.

623.8224 22   VM321.52.C2M655 2005

Library and Archives Canada Cataloguing in Publication

Mollica, Anthony S., 1932–
Classic boats of the Thousand Islands / Anthony Mollica Jr. ;photography by George Fischer.

Includes bibliographical references and index.
ISBN 1-55046-441-8

1. Boats and boating — Thousand Islands Region (N.Y. and Ont.) — History.
2. Boatbuilding — Thousand Islands Region (N.Y. and Ont.) — History.
3. Boats and boating — Thousand Islands Region (N.Y. and Ont.) — Pictorial works.
4. Thousand Islands Region (N.Y. and Ont.) — History. I. Fischer, George,1954– II. Title.

GV776.15.T48M64 2005   797.1'09713'7
C2004-906959-4

Contents

Introduction

I t is not unusual for experienced travelers to insist that the Thousand Islands region of the St. Lawrence River is one of the most spectacular and picturesque vistas that they've ever encountered. For boating enthusiasts the Thousand Islands is a marvelous recreational waterway, providing virtually everything desired for a wonderful adventure on the water. The beauty of the islands and crystal-clear water of the river constantly amaze visitors. And the wide variety of watercraft, from small rowing skiffs to huge ocean-going freighters and luxury cruise ships, adds more to delight tourists and boaters. All this within a few hours' drive for a significant portion of the continent's population.

The Thousand Islands region actually begins at the northeastern end of Lake Ontario. Here, the fresh water of all five Great Lakes makes its final journey to the North Atlantic via the St. Lawrence River. The mouth of the river is located between the city of Kingston, Ontario, in Canada, and the village of Cape Vincent, in northern New York State. Here, along the first 50 miles of the St. Lawrence River, lie the more than 1,800 islands responsible for the region's descriptive name. The islands vary in size from tiny granite formations with two trees to islands large enough to support commercial farms and thriving summer communities.

From Lake Ontario, the St. Lawrence River flows steadily northeast for more than 700 miles before entering the Atlantic Ocean north of Nova Scotia. Its broad opening offered early explorers an enticing entry that penetrated deep into the North American continent. Jacques Cartier was the first of several French explorers who journeyed boldly along the great river. It was on August 10, 1534, a date celebrated by the French to commemorate Saint Lawrence, that Cartier actually entered the river for the first time. As a man of strong faith, Cartier believed it fortuitous to name the river for the highly regarded saint and thereby provide his

In this recreation of a vintage photo, Baby Gar V *speeds past Boldt Castle.*

expedition with a much-needed blessing. Indeed, his journey was successful, covering nearly 500 miles and ending at the future site of the great city of Montreal. It was here that swift rapids finally prevented his large ship from proceeding any farther upriver. It would be several years before any other European explorers would travel beyond the rapids, using much smaller craft to discover the area of the Thousand Islands, Lake Ontario and the other Great Lakes beyond.

Years later, another French explorer, Samuel de Champlain, would successfully establish permanent settlements along the shores of the St. Lawrence River. Champlain would be remembered as the first European to travel into the area that would become known as the Thousand Islands. Here, the myriad islands and channels present a remarkable contrast to the rest of the river and to Lake Ontario, where island formations are relatively scarce. The geologic makeup of the islands is mostly solid granite and sandstone. After the last ice sheets melted some 10,000 years ago, the torrential runoff cleared a path through the St. Lawrence Valley and resulted in the present island formations.

The five Great Lakes flow from the center of the North American continent eastward towards the mouth of the St. Lawrence River. It is here, at the mouth of the river, that the world's largest reservoir of fresh water begins its final 750-mile journey to the Atlantic Ocean.

In the mid-1800s the Thousand Islands region was rediscovered as a marvelous haven for sportsmen. Perhaps the event most responsible for its rediscovery was a well-publicized visit by Ulysses S. Grant, President of United States, in 1872. Word of his fishing success spread, inciting huge numbers of travelers and sportsmen to see this wonderful region for themselves. Virtually overnight the Thousand Islands became one of North America's most active tourist destinations. The railroads seized upon the growing interest and provided passenger service from major eastern cities to the prospering villages along the river. Large hotels were quickly under construction to meet the demand from the ever-growing number of visitors who wanted to experience the area for themselves.

Among the earliest boats developed specifically for the prevailing water conditions was a double-ended rowing craft that would become known as the St. Lawrence skiff. Its efficiently designed hull featured overlapping cedar planks, making it ideal for rowing easily around and through the channels and bays created by the islands. The skiff design also proved to be very suitable for local fishing guides. The guides became skilled at building skiffs themselves or with the help of a friend during the winter season. The basic design was so successful that it became universally accepted, with only slight variations among the individual builders.

The small craft was perfectly suited for livery operators to rent by the hour or day to visitors. For fishing guides, the skiff provided their customers with a comfortable day-long fishing experience that might include several miles of rowing. As the demand for skiffs increased, commercial boatbuilding firms began to produce large numbers of St. Lawrence skiffs in various lengths with thoughtful custom features. There was a time when nearly every home along the river had at least one skiff at their disposal.

As glowing reports of the region spread, construction of summer homes along the mainland shore and on the islands grew steadily. At first the river homes were modest cottages or fishing lodges. Soon, however, the summer homes grew larger, more elaborate and some even spectacular. Wealthy summer residents acquired large steam yachts to provide their houseguests with personalized cruises among the islands. Rapidly the Thousand Islands became the most talked about and prestigious boating mecca in North America.

Monitor, the 38-foot 1906 Hutchinson launch approaches its home port on beautiful Pullman Island.

In addition to owning luxurious yachts and skiffs, boaters became involved in the new sport of motorboat racing. The remarkable success of Thousand Islands yacht clubs in racing competition encouraged the development of several state-of-the-art boatbuilding shops in the river communities. Many of the great racing champions of the 1920s and 1930s traveled to the Thousand Islands to compete. Even now, the Antique Boat Museum in Clayton, New York, continues to host the popular Antique Race Boat Regatta, featuring famous raceboats from the past. This special event is held every two years and always attracts thousands of boaters, who marvel at the beautiful classic raceboats from a bygone era that are still capable of exciting high-speed performances.

However, when speedboat performances advanced well beyond the capabilities of the weekend gentleman driver, serious racing gradually faded on the river. Successful speedboat racing became the domain of professional drivers, and local boatbuilders focused their attention on building boats better suited to the needs of the summer boaters. Sport utility boats and motorized guideboats were among the more popular designs as interest in fishing continued. The sport-utility boats were swift yet soft-riding. They were comfortable and well suited to the needs of sportsmen, with bait wells, fish-holding tanks, folding windshields and comfortable seating arrangements.

This book highlights many of the wonderful classic boats that have survived the test of time and still operate faithfully along one of North America's most attractive and historic waterways. On any given day, classic mahogany boats comfortably transport their owners to a favorite restaurant, to an island house party, or to a reliable fishing spot where a big bass might be waiting. Appropriately enough, it was right in the Thousand Islands that the very first antique boat show was organized and

Night Rider, a Thousand Islands one-design racer built by Joseph Leyare in 1909.

conducted some 40 years ago. It was the success of this boat show that resulted in the hundreds of antique boat shows that now take place every summer in North America. Perhaps the most significant result of that first boat show was the development of the Antique Boat Museum in Clayton, now recognized as the premier museum of its type in the world.

Although this book only captures a few of the hundreds of classic boats of the Thousand Islands, the selected examples show the interesting diversity of types, including some that have become part of the river culture. Some boats are maintained in pristine condition and are capable of winning awards in boat shows with just a few minutes' notice. Others are reliable boats in regular service all season that are maintained in excellent running condition, yet show telltale signs of their extensive use. All, however, are well-suited to the daily needs of their present owners.

Whenever possible, the boats were photographed near the boathouses that they normally occupy or near the homes of their present or former owners. The settings provide a logical association for readers between the boat and its connection to the land. In some cases the story of the owner's acquisition of the boat and their residency in the islands provides a compelling tale in its own right — most owners of classic boats have a long and colorful history of boating, and their love of fine boats and of boating in the Thousand Islands seems to be unshakable. This book is intended to provide readers with a glimpse of the active classic boats that continue to perform the tasks that they were designed to carry out decades ago, and still look attractive doing it.

While every effort was made to include noteworthy examples, there are simply too many interesting classic boats in the Thousand Islands to claim anything close to complete success. Scheduling challenges, the availability of boat owners and suitable weather conditions for photography are just a few of the circumstances that influenced the ultimate inclusion of boats in this book.

Zipalong, a 1936 18-foot Gar Wood runabout.

A North American Treasure

The natural basin that feeds the five Great Lakes of North America drains nearly 700,000 square miles of the interior of the continent. All of the surface water in this gigantic basin flows into the five lakes and eventually into the St. Lawrence River. The lakes act as a series of settling bowls that naturally remove the silt gathered from their tributaries, a natural process that eventually provides the river with sparkling clear water. The enormous watershed is such an abundantly reliable source of water that the level of the river remains remarkably constant throughout the year. This is a feature rarely found in any other major river system around the world; all too often, the other great rivers are capable of destructive floods during their rainy seasons or run dry in times of drought.

The portion of the river known as the Thousand Islands begins at the river's mouth and extends about 50 miles downriver. The maze of tree-covered islands is so concentrated that the international boundary line between the United States and Canada becomes virtually indistinguishable. The island formations are like a series of friendly stepping stones that blur the border for boaters and fishermen traveling on the river. The size, shape and overall appearance of the islands is remarkably varied, and the larger islands are able to support substantial farms and year-round residents. The smaller islands provide their residents with a unique sanctuary like no other place on Earth.

For nearly 200 years the Native American Iroquois occupied this region. They referred to it as their "Garden of the Great Spirit." It was in the Thousand Islands, Iroquois legend holds, that Hiawatha first appeared before the Confederacy of the Five Nations.

The first river inhabitants from Lake Ontario to Lake Champlain were the Oneida; however, when the Algonquin migrated into the region, problems between the two nations

A.C.S., a superb 35-foot 1931 Hutchinson,
follows an old island tradition of having its owner's initials as its name.

resulted in constant battles. In 1535 Jacques Cartier explored the lower St. Lawrence River Valley and boldly claimed all of what he saw for France. He believed that this route would eventually lead to China and named the rapids he encountered *La Chine*, French for China. He soon became convinced, however, that it was not a new passage to China, but a route to the interior of a vast continent.

Years later, in 1615, Cartier's route was followed by Samuel de Champlain, another well-respected French explorer. Using bark canoes, Champlain traveled over the rapids that had prevented Cartier from extending his exploration past the present site of Montreal. When Champlain's small group explored the region of the Thousand Islands it was sparsely inhabited, yet there were still territorial battles going on between the Oneida and the Algonquin.

Champlain finally chose to support the Algonquin, and this decision was all that was necessary for the Iroquois Confederacy to permanently consider the French as their enemy, eventually helping to precipitate the French and Indian War.

In the meantime the Five Nations of the Iroquois successfully migrated to the Lake Region in the central part of what is now New York State. The land north of their new settlements, all the way to the St. Lawrence River, was used primarily for hunting and fishing; they had little interest in establishing permanent settlements there.

Geologically, the islands that are collectively referred to as the Thousand Islands are simply the uppermost peaks of granite and sandstone that rise from the depths of the river bottom. The melting glaciers created a torrential runoff that washed away all of the loose

rock and soil, leaving only the harder granite peaks that are the present islands. The carving action caused by the glacial runoff frequently resulted in sharp drop-offs along the shoreline of many islands. This results in relatively deep water close to edges of the islands, which allows boats to navigate remarkably close to the shore. The close proximity provides touring boaters with unusually intimate glimpses of beautiful summer homes and their gardens.

The abundance and variety of the islands is so appealing that it is easy to be captivated by their charm. Visitors often ask local residents how they differentiate between a small island and a big shoal that is exposed just above the surface. The most frequent response is that the rock formation in question must be above the water for the entire year and must also support two trees. Otherwise, it's simply a shoal!

The river's swift movement provides an important and dependable source of hydroelectric power. It has also become one of the world's great commercial thoroughfares. Its considerable depth of water provides a route directly into North America's heartland and major population centers. Altogether, the Great Lakes and the St. Lawrence River span half of the continent and drain the watersheds of seventeen states and four Canadian provinces.

By the beginning of the nineteenth century the Thousand Islands region was settled by trappers, hunters and commercial fishermen. Soon afterwards ferry service was established, connecting Clayton's Bartlett Point in the U.S. across the border to Gananoque, Ontario. The Canadian frontier was so poorly guarded that smuggling across the border was rampant, as illegal trading of all kinds of goods was easy and very profitable. Government agents were so few that smugglers practically ruled the region unchallenged.

After the War of 1812, however, a more responsible law-abiding attitude prevailed as the value of commercial lumber flourished and it emerged as the dominant industry. The river's reliable current allowed loggers to make huge rafts of freshly cut timber that they could guide downriver all the way to Montreal. Here the demand was high, and the profit to loggers substantial. Commerce expanded, and the demand for more shipbuilding soared.

With the signing of the Porter–Barclay Treaty in 1822, the United States and Canada established the international boundary and ownership of the islands. Islands that fell on the American side of the boundary line were legally assigned to Jefferson County, in New York State. The state, in turn, sold nearly all of its islands to Colonel Elisha Camp and an investment firm. Twenty-three years later, a merchant from Alexandria Bay paid $3,000 for nearly all of the islands on the American side of the boundary. His plan was to systematically strip each island of its timber to supply fuel for the ever-increasing number of steamships moving passengers and goods along the river. The new enterprise flourished, and after each island was completely stripped of its useable timber and rendered barren, it was offered for sale to individual owners for development.

Early island owners built docks, skiff ramps, small cabins and primitive hunting lodges on their new properties. The domed topography of the islands also offered a tempting natural pedestal that appealed to the creativity of some island owners. There were no

Charming Thousand Island stick cottages.

rules to follow, and it wasn't long before some of the wealthier islanders began to erect structures that were far more than a simple summer retreat. The remarkable beauty of the islands seemed to foster unusual creativity in even the most conservative islanders.

The inspiration to build innovative structures was contagious, and this soon became the accepted type of construction among the more affluent summer families. The abundance of building stone and plentiful lumber, along with inexpensive skilled labor, added to the creativity. Island construction presents unusual difficulties for both builder and owner; however, the extra complexity associated with island construction seemed to make the results even more satisfying for the owners. Before the end of the nineteenth century the Thousand Islands would be North America's most appealing summer playground.

Unquestionably, the first great boost to interest in the region was the 1872 presidential visit, during which President Ulysses S. Grant spent a week vacationing with George Pullman on his island near Alexandria Bay. Pullman was the highly successful manufacturer of the railroad passenger car of the same name that provided comfortable sleeping accommodations for overnight passengers. Every fish the President caught made the national news, and he caught plenty. The period immediately following the President's stay at Pullman Island is historically referred to as "the Rush of '72." And it was exactly that — a rush to see the storied location where the fish had virtually jumped into the President's boat. The entourage of reporters following the President wrote glowingly about the region's natural beauty and the

President's abundant catches of pike and bass, and in an instant the entire nation was introduced to the natural wonders of the Thousand Islands. That was all it took — everyone was now determined to see this attractive setting as soon as they could.

Although it was not an easy place for most people to reach, the visitors who made it there loved what they experienced, and as word spread the popularity of the region was set for decades to follow. The railroads quickly improved their summer schedules and built extra spurs to bring several trains each day right to the steamship docks in Clayton and Cape Vincent. During the peak summer months there were a dozen or more trains destined each day for the Thousand Islands.

George Pullman knew that it was time for him to replace his delicate, two-story, wood-frame fishing lodge with something a bit grander; he wanted to do something tasteful but spectacular on his lovely 3.5-acre island. The new structure, named Castle Rest, was completed in time for the summer of 1888,

Boldt Castle on Heart Island.

and it *was* spectacular. More than that, Castle Rest set a new standard of excellence for island residences.

In 1893 tobacco merchant Charles Emery, one of the principal founders of the American Tobacco Company, built his red sandstone castle on Calumet Island, across from Clayton. George Boldt, famous proprietor of New York's finest hotel, the Waldorf-Astoria, followed suit with his spectacular (but unfinished) castle in 1900. Not to be outdone, Frederick Bourne, president of the Singer Sewing Machine Company, completed his castle on Dark Island in 1906. The

Thousand Islands had firmly established itself as North America's summer playground for wealthy boaters.

This unprecedented development spawned a wide range of service industries in the region. The small river communities flourished with services and business activity, as there was steady demand for highly skilled stonecutters, masons, carpenters, steelworkers and boatbuilders. Lumber yards, quarries, hotels and restaurants opened and thrived.

By the turn of the century, powerboat racing was becoming the latest interest of the wealthy barons of summer on the river. For nine consecutive years, from 1904 to 1912, a member of one of the four Thousand Islands' yacht clubs was awarded boating's most prestigious symbol for sustained speed on the water, the Gold Cup trophy. Yacht clubs became the social activity centers for summer residents and yachtsmen.

In reality, the multitude of stories related to summer homes and their owners is filled with successes, failures, creativity and even absurdity. Yet it is truly remarkable that so many island structures have survived for more than a hundred years in spite of depressions, world wars, gasoline rationing and even decades of total neglect. The Thousand Islands have been rediscovered once again by boaters, sportsmen, tourists and summer residents. It remains one of North America's greatest treasures, where the water is clear, the sportfishing wonderful, the natural features spectacular, and the recreational boating marvelous.

Boatbuilding
in the Thousand Islands

T he early European explorers sailed upriver in their large ships as far as the Lachine
Rapids. The only way to proceed farther was to build much smaller craft that would be
suitable for negotiating the swift and perilous turbulence of the rapids, and at the same
time able to carry needed supplies. As a result, boatbuilding grew of necessity, and it soon
flourished all along the river.

By the middle of the nineteenth century, boatbuilding in the Thousand Islands region was
becoming a thriving industry. Commercial fishing, logging, ferry service, passenger service and
individual fishing guides all required specialized boats to meet their discrete needs. One unique
outcome of this regional boatbuilding activity was the St. Lawrence skiff.

There are differing opinions as to exactly where the St. Lawrence skiff originated. Some
historians suspect it was derived from early northern European rowing craft of lapstrake construction. Others say its beginnings were in Brockville, Ontario, while still others trace the skiff's
origin to Clayton, New York. Whatever the location, it was the splendid suitability of this round-
bottom, lapstrake, double-ended rowboat, as well as its timely appearance, that assured enduring
success. As noted by naval architect and marine historian Howard Chapelle: "Designers have
always borrowed ideas from each other. It is important to keep this in mind when considering the
St. Lawrence skiff, because it is so unusual a rowboat that people commonly assume someone
must have invented it. Even local boatbuilders often wondered who built the first one."

Most studies suggest that the origin may have been Canadian. In the early 1800s there
were nearly three times more Canadians living along the St. Lawrence River than New
Yorkers. It is also true that many of the new Canadians were former New Englanders skilled in

The 33-foot 1956 Futura Express Cruiser introduced an exciting new design trend for Chris-Craft.

shipbuilding. During the War of 1812 many of them built schooners, scows and dories.

Historian John Keats wrote of the St. Lawrence skiff, "It was a workboat, and a family boat, just as necessary to an island farmer in the nineteenth century as an automobile is necessary to a suburban commuter today. But the skiff is, and always was something more than a mere workboat. Its design is at once indigenous and unique. The boat first appeared only in the Thousand Islands region of the St. Lawrence River and nowhere else along the river's 750 miles from Lake Ontario to the sea. No marine architect ever sat down to a drawing board to design the skiff. The boat evolved in response to pioneer needs with respect to local marine conditions."

It was a time when sportsmen were becoming aware of enthusiastic reports of great catches of fish from the Thousand Islands. Railroads and steamships were beginning to respond to the heightened tourist interest to provide convenient transportation access into the area. Before long, improved transportation was helping thousands of visitors to travel into the region for the first time. The St. Lawrence skiff was quickly recognized as an ideal boat with which local fishing guides could take one, two or more paying clients to a favorite location for a memorable fishing experience. The catches lived up to expectations, and the fishing guides flourished. The St. Lawrence skiffs were comfortable, stable in rough water and much faster than the conventional rowboats. The skiff has remarkable stability for its size and weight — a heavy man can lean over the side to net a large fish without fear of

A 1900 St. Lawrence skiff,
a 1909 long-deck launch and a 1932 runabout.

overturning the craft, and the relatively low freeboard at midships facilitates bringing the large fish aboard quickly. The skilled fishing guide, who was also the oarsman, might row several miles during an outing to satisfy his client's desire for an abundant catch of fish. The skiff design provided a craft that was comfortable, seaworthy and swift. It was ideal for guides and equally suited for their patrons.

Almost overnight, small shops sprang up throughout the region on both sides of the river, busily building St. Lawrence skiffs to meet the growing demand. The builders expanded their offerings with a variety of lengths, from the small "Ladies skiff" to the larger 20-foot and 22-foot touring models. The skiffs were available with basic painted hulls or varnished hulls, with choices of more exotic woods and fancy trim. A. Bain & Company in Clayton constructed a three story factory in order to increase production capability and keep up with the others building skiffs.

The development of the internal combustion gasoline engine was quickly followed by the installation of gasoline engines in boats. One of the earliest sports for the new motorboaters was racing. Early boat racing was not always fast; however, it turned out to be an excellent way for engine manufacturers to test the endurance and reliability of their products. All of the early boat races were promoted and sponsored by leading automobile manufacturers.

The yachtsmen of the Thousand Islands were among the first to become interested in racing motorboats. In 1903 the American Power Boat Association was formed for the express purpose of promoting speed trials to improve the development of engines and the design of boats — boat racing had a specific industrial goal. The new organization commissioned Tiffany to fashion a suitable trophy for the annual winner. It was known as the Gold Cup.

One of the interesting traditions in boat racing is that the winner of the event is given the opportunity to defend their title on home waters. So when Jonathan Wainright's raceboat, *Chip*, won the 1905 Gold Cup trophy, he moved the 1906 race to the Chippewa Bay Yacht Club in the Thousand Islands. For the following eight years a raceboat from one of the Thousand Islands yacht clubs kept hold of the Gold Cup trophy. And each year the winner's club would host the race during the following season. This early domination of the prestigious Gold Cup races drew even more sportsmen to the Thousand Islands. It also helped accelerate the growing interest among regional boatbuilders in focusing on the development of fast boats and powerful engines.

The commuter A.C.S. *waits at the end of the walk.*

The Thousand Islands was emerging as North America's premier boating playground, with creative writers calling it the "Venice of North America." Its popularity expanded in unison with the rising wealth in the eastern regions of the two nations. Interested tourists could purchase a round-trip ticket aboard a comfortable Pullman sleeping car leaving New York City after work on Friday for less than $20. They could have dinner on the train and wake up in Clayton for breakfast on Saturday morning, then enjoy two full days at a fine hotel in "America's Venice" before boarding the return sleeper to New York, arriving in time for work on Monday morning.

In the peak season there were a dozen trains arriving each day in Clayton; the journey from New York City to Clayton in the last quarter of the nineteenth century was more convenient to accomplish than it is today.

During the years when motorboating was growing in popularity, many wealthy sportsmen spent their summers in the Thousand Islands. This was a time when great wealth could be generated at unprecedented rates for vast numbers of entrepreneurs, and the new rich built spectacular summer homes and ordered huge yachts. It was also a time before boat designs were standardized and boat construction took place along production lines. In the Thousand Islands it was commonplace for a boat buyer to confer directly with owners at Hutchinson Brothers, Duclon, Cupernall, Adams, or Fitzgerald & Lee to discuss their ideas for their next boat. The boatbuilders would begin with sketches and then prepare plans based upon the buyer's suggestions for their anticipated boating activities. When the details were completed, the new one-of-a-kind boat would be fashioned specifically for the owner.

Many of the new boat buyers were also island residents. They favored swift, comfortable, commuter-style boats operated by their hired captain. Other islanders preferred smaller sporty boats well suited to scoot or run about from one gala island party to another. It was here, in the Thousand Islands, that the term "runabout" became so universally associated with swift sport boats, and before long the name was adopted by the boating industry.

Another design type well suited to the river was the guide's launch. This soft-riding boat was wonderful for day-long fishing parties, with plenty of room for the owner's guests and a knowledgeable guide to fulfill their quest for all the game fish they could eat. As hull designs improved to take advantage of more powerful engines, the displacement-style launch was eventually replaced by the advanced sport-utility design.

Having a custom-built boat constructed by one of the local boatbuilders was the accepted norm for many Thousand Islanders, as buyers were able to build to suit their individual needs. Regional boatbuilders offered superb craftsmanship and all the services required to maintain the boats properly year after year. Individual builders took great pride in their special construction details, and each plank of tropical hardwood was carefully selected and matched to provide the finishers with a hull that would gleam in the sunlight like a fine piece of furniture. Frequently, the prospective owner would make the arrangements for building the new boat during his summer sojourn in the islands. Usually the new boat would be completed by the following spring and ready to use during the next season.

After the Depression years, some of the larger Thousand Islands boatbuilders used the designs of independent naval architects. As the power of marine engines improved, superior hull performance required advanced technical skills. John Hacker emerged as one of the favorite custom designers for both Hutchinson and Fitzgerald & Lee. In the 1930s, Hutchinson Boat Works used Hacker designs for a

Kon Tiki's boathouse reflected in the spotlight.

special series of standardized triple-cockpit runabouts as well as other custom designs. Fitzgerald & Lee produced a wide range of Hacker custom designs, including *Vamoose I* and *Vamoose II*, which were high-performance commuters for Charles Lyons. After the conclusion of the Second World War, Hutchinson accepted Lyon's contract to build what is considered one of Hacker's best-known runabouts, *Pardon Me*.

Hutchinson also built outstanding sport-utilities in two popular lengths: the 22-footer and the 26-footer. The hulls reflected time-tested evolutionary refinements to provide exceptionally soft, level-riding performance in rough water conditions. The early hulls were mostly of lapstrake construction. After the Second World War, however, most of the hulls were produced with carvel planking, which formed a smooth hull surface more in keeping with the contemporary buyer's desire for more modern styling. The post-war Hutchinson sport-utilities offered greater beam, exceptional flare, wide covering boards, a modern stem and a superbly designed, mahogany-framed windshield. Their most innovative treatment, however, was the addition of a hard chine to their traditional soft-riding rounded hull. It was a successful demonstration of the high-quality craftsmanship that always existed in Hutchinson's talented staff of boat carpenters. Their sport-utility continued to provide the traditional soft ride associated with round bilge hulls. At speeds above 22 mph their innovative hard chine provided the extra lift to take advantage of the engine's power to achieve higher speeds and level riding performance. It was another significant achievement that received little recognition beyond the St. Lawrence River boaters.

As America was drawn into the Second World War, Fitzgerald & Lee ended production of new boats, and their skilled craftsmen went to work for the Hutchinson Boat Works, which had major defense contracts assigned to them. Hutchinson's work force grew to nearly 175 men, producing more than 20 large military craft for the armed services. After the successful conclusion of the war, Fitzgerald & Lee's superb boat shop never resumed production.

Hutchinson Boat Works was fully prepared at the war's end to restart peacetime production of 22-foot and 26-foot deluxe sport-utilities, as well as custom boats. One of the first custom orders received was from Charles Lyons. His two high-performance commuters, *Vamoose I* and *II*, were both well known in the Thousand Islands and nationally; however, Lyons was ready for something even more spectacular. This time he asked John Hacker to design a truly super runabout that could handle one of the powerful 1,800-horsepower, 12-cylinder Packard PT boat engines produced by Packard Motors during the war. Hacker's design would be the 47-foot runabout known throughout the boating world as *Pardon Me*.

The design and construction of *Pardon Me* by Hutchinson was flawless. It is one of the best-known runabouts ever built; however, there were a series of initial mechanical and hydraulic challenges that frustrated both Hacker and Lyons with its operation and performance. It would take the additional creativity and resourcefulness of a succession of owners to solve the early challenges. It remains today one of the finest boatbuilding achievements of its

The 30-foot Hutchinson launch C.D.S., built in 1914.

type, drawing crowds of admirers to the Antique Boat Museum, where it permanently resides. (In an act of great generosity, the last owner, Jim Lewis, donated *Pardon Me* to the museum.) A few years ago the museum decided to launch *Pardon Me* to demonstrate its thrilling performance for special contributors. The boat did not disappoint any of the scores of participants, and everyone claimed that its performance was everything they hoped it might be.

In the years immediately following the Second World War, Hutchinson restored a number of cruisers that had been drafted by the military for patrol service. The cruisers were painted military gray and modified for their special duties. In addition to this work, Hutchinson was constructing 14 to 20 boats a year, including custom orders. This number might include eight or nine 22-foot sport-utilities and four or five 26-foot sport-utilities.

In 1952 Bert Hutchinson died, and his estate sold the business to Cyriel Heath and Glen Furness, who were already associated with the firm. Heath was an outstanding craftsman, and Furness was an equally talented naval architect. It was a strong combination, and Hutchinson continued to build boats through to 1964, when their sport-utility production finally ended. They continued to build a few steel workboats until 1967. From this point on they specialized in repairing boats, refinishing and storage. Today, Hutchinson operates an extensive marina facility in two locations and is a major dealer for contemporary boat manufacturers.

The St. Lawrence Skiff
and Other Light Craft

There was a time when nearly every dwelling along the river owned at least one St. Lawrence skiff, which was safely secured on a ramp or in a skiff house. The skiff was the most reliable form of river transportation for every family, and each family member knew how to use it. Whether fishing, hauling, sailing or cruising, the family skiff was always ready for service.

Even today many river households still have a St. Lawrence skiff in the boathouse or resting on a ramp, ready to row quietly around the islands. The joy of skiffing remains one of the special treats enjoyed by families living along the river. Some of the skiffs on the river are a hundred years old or older. Many are just 60 or 70 years old, and a few are even new. The new skiffs still have the same lines as the vintage skiffs, though. There are even a few fiberglass skiffs that were molded directly from the hull of one of the oldest wooden skiffs in the Antique Boat Museum. But the traditional skiff design doesn't need to be altered or improved — there's a special feeling when rowing or sailing the St. Lawrence skiff because the hull is near perfection in form and function, with smooth, graceful lines.

During the winter, fishing guides, craftsmen and farmers built skiffs to use or to sell the following summer. Many of the larger riverfront hotels operated skiff liveries for the convenience of their guests, who relished the opportunity to fish and explore the islands in these responsive craft. Over time, the popularity of the St. Lawrence skiff spread far beyond the Thousand Islands, and commercial boatbuilding firms began to offer them in their sales catalogs. The Skaneateles Boat Company, a major builder of small craft, offered six different models of the skiff in their 1919 catalog. Soon builders throughout New England and as far west as Michigan were offering these popular craft.

Although the basic St. Lawrence skiff design remained virtually unchanged, variations included sailing versions. In 1882 Monty Atwood, a plumber from Clayton, designed and patented his version

Six St. Lawrence skiffs ready for service in the skiff Livery at the Antique Boat Museum.

of the folding centerboard. It folded like a lady's fan and fit efficiently into a surprisingly compact trunk located neatly under one of the middle seats. This sailing version of the skiff was equipped with a circular opening in the forward deck for the mast, which fit into a recess in the keel. When under sail, the skiff sailors did not need a rudder to turn their boat; the technique for turning or coming about was unusual but quite effective. It was the design of the skiff itself, as well as the skipper's skill, that made turning possible without a rudder. When it was necessary to turn, the skipper would move forward in the skiff, raising the centerboard as he passed by. As he moved forward, the bow would dip deeper and the stern would rise, thus catching the wind. The wind would swing the stern around and the skipper would return aft, lowering the centerboard once more as he passed by. Then he trimmed his sail and proceeded on the new tack.

Most of the skiffs use a single mainsail with a simple sprit rig. This setup requires a four-sided sail that is held out from the mast by a narrow, lightweight spar called a sprit. It is usually the same length as the mast and supports the sail at its peak, or the head of the sail. The base of the sprit is secured near the base of the mast, extending upwards to the sail's outermost corner to provide the proper amount of tension. This arrangement allows more sail area for a given mast length. The sprit rig is quite easy for one person to set up and handle — there is no need for stays or shrouds to support the skiff's mast. Once underway, the skipper has only two lines to manage. One is the sheet that trims the sail and the other line is the snotter to correctly position the sprit to help form the most efficient shape of the sail.

As the popularity of skiff sailing increased, more skiffs were offered with folding centerboards and mast openings in the foredeck. Fishing guides often participated in sailing races at the end of the season to demonstrate their skill at rudderless sailing. The guides of Clayton and the guides of Gananoque frequently challenged each other to see which community possessed the finest skiff sailors. The special art of skiff sailing is still popular along the river, with a traditional trophy race held each summer during Clayton's annual Antique Boat Show.

Another variation that appeared was a motorized version of the skiff, which was affectionately referred to as the Skiff-Putt. It was, to all appearances, a traditional skiff with a small inboard gasoline engine that drove a shaft to the propeller. A rudder was mounted on the stern using rope-and-pulley steering. However, by the time the Skiff-Putt was introduced, the development of the small motorboat was progressing very rapidly. With advanced engine development, a wide range of design options with greater overall performance and innovative styling became possible for builders to consider.

The most popular size for the St. Lawrence skiff was the 18-foot length, followed by the 16-footer. However, the 20- and 22-foot lengths provided greater capacity, rowed smoothly and were generally quite a bit faster than the shorter lengths. The longer skiffs did, however, require greater turning distances. Typically, fishing guides preferred the longer-length skiffs for both capacity and quickness. The majority of the American skiff hulls were built with overlapping cedar planks that formed a stepped hull, although some builders offered skiffs with smooth planking rather than lapstrake style. More of the Canadian builders offered smooth-hulled skiffs that they were able to create by beveling the strakes onto each other. This technique also provides more surface contact with the ribs and strakes. The overlapping strakes provide the hull with excellent tracking characteristics and a measure of additional lift when rowing in choppy waves.

Although the overall shape and design of the skiffs was remarkably similar, each builder incorporated enough subtle variations to clearly present a craft that was unique. Variations were

A sample of the creative deck detailing that was common to St. Lawrence skiffs.

even present among hulls from the same builder. Builders used a set of molds to facilitate planking the skiff hulls, and there are no surviving records showing that skiff builders ever used construction drawings or blueprints. The mold was a strong wooden frame that established the shape of the hull they were about to build. It began with an oak strongback that was the length of the boat. Upon this strongback were fastened a series of wooden templates or forms that were placed at precise intervals to establish a framework upon which the hull would be planked. The layout of the forms determined the final shape and length of the hull. The mold, as it was called, was propped up above the shop floor by supports so that it was placed at a suitable height to facilitate the planking procedure.

The first step was to place the oak keel onto the molds and bolt the stems to it. After the keel was firmly in place, the planking would begin with the garboard planks (the first planks on either side of the keel). The edge of the garboard strake would fit into a groove cut into the keel. The next strake would overlap the garboard strake, creating an edge similar to the way clapboard siding overlaps on the exterior of a house. The hull was completely planked upside down on the mold. Typically, a skiff had six or seven strakes on each side, and though the skiff hull appeared to be identical at each end, the aft end (where the chair seat is placed) was slightly fuller. This obscure construction detail provided additional buoyancy to the hull when a fishing guide had just one person aboard in the aft seat. With most skiff builders the beam of the skiff remained constant at 42 inches, even though the length of the skiff might vary anywhere from 12 feet to 22 feet.

The St. Lawrence skiff Juanita *and passenger.*

At this point in construction the hull was completely formed on the mold without any ribs in place. The builder carefully marked each location where the ribs were to be located. Usually, ribs were 5 or 6 inches apart, perpendicular to the keel over the entire length of the hull. This spacing would require more than 40 ribs in a typical 18-foot skiff, based upon 5-inch intervals. At this point the hull was ready to be removed from the mold, turned right side up and ribbed.

The ribs were strips of oak or elm that required steam bending to properly fit the contours of their respective stations inside the hull. When sufficiently steamed, the ribs became astonishingly flexible, but only for a very brief time. This step usually required two men working together. One had to remove a rib from the steamer and quickly bend it to the contour in its precise location while his partner secured it in place with clinch nails or rivets. The entire process had to be completed in seconds or the rib would quickly become rigid once more. With the ribs successfully fastened, the hull was stabilized and ready for the builder to proceed with the decking, seats and varnishing or painting.

The gunwales were often built up of contrasting shades of hardwoods that could be quite spectacular when varnished. The finished hull was very rigid, quite strong and weighed about 175 to 190 pounds. Skiff builders offered a wide range of exotic hardwoods

The typical interior of a St. Lawrence skiff.

that they would use for the decks, seat trim and ceiling liners to meet the customer's wishes. As a result, skiffs often had just enough unique variations to make each one slightly different and rather special. The woods frequently used included black cherry, butternut, black walnut, mahogany, bird's eye and tiger maple. The oars were usually 7 or 7.5 feet long, made of white ash. The skiff oars pivoted on thole pins rather than oar horns, which often puzzled first-time users. The basic reason for the thole pin oars was that the prime purpose of the skiff was fishing. When a fish strikes, the oarsman or guide will simply release the oars, pick up the landing net and tend quickly to the catch. The released oars naturally swing alongside the hull and out of the landing net's path.

The length of time it took to build a skiff varied greatly and depended on many factors. Individual fishing guides might build one or two skiffs over an entire winter season. A skilled builder, however, with a well-equipped shop and a part-time helper, could turn out an 18-foot skiff in two weeks, before paint and varnish were applied. The finishing phase, where weather conditions controlled the drying time, could take as long as the construction phase for individual builders. Commercial skiff-building shops were well equipped and could paint and varnish several skiffs at one time in heated finishing rooms, thus significantly reducing the finishing time.

Juanita, *a 100-year-old painted St. Lawrence skiff, was likely built by a fishing guide for his own use.*

Juanita

Juanita is one of many St. Lawrence skiffs constructed by an unknown craftsman. This skiff has no nameplate, nor is there a hull number, nor any single feature that has helped the present owner identify its builder. More than likely, a local fishing guide built it during the winter season. From a historical perspective, *Juanita* is very important because she is one of the most authentic St. Lawrence skiffs. Skiffs built by guides would often be painted and be devoid of fancy trim. There would be a logical reason and purpose for each feature built into a working guide's skiff to help them be more efficient as a guide.

It is believed that *Juanita* was built in a small shed in or near Alexandria Bay and followed designs that were commonly shared among the local guides. Most of the construction for *Juanita* was the work of one craftsman. When help was required, a friend would be called to assist. There was a lot of cooperation among the local skiff builders who helped each other and shared their boatbuilding methods. *Juanita* possesses the traditional length, beam, depth, weight and style typical of the time. In some ways, the fact that her builder didn't use a nameplate may be consistent with her origin as the product of a working guide.

Securely slid onto her ramp along the shore,
Juanita *is sheltered and ready to be launched again quickly.*

Many St. Lawrence skiffs used attractive plaques
on either side of the bow to highlight their names.

Blue Bill

A 19-FOOT ST. LAWRENCE SKIFF

A ride in the chairback aft seat is a very pleasant way to enjoy a quiet morning in the Thousand Islands.

The 75-year-old Dowsett St. Lawrence skiff Blue Bill *still serves her owners well, though showing some signs of her frequent use.*

B*lue Bill* is a double-oared St. Lawrence skiff built by W. J. Dowsett in Portland, Ontario, in the early 1930s. At 19 feet, the overall length is a bit unusual for the skiffs, which were usually 18 or 20 feet. However, each boat was individually built to meet the builder's own specifications, and since this is a double-oared model, the original owner, Major Clifford Sifton, may have had a special purpose in mind — perhaps using the skiff with another oarsperson. If this were the case, perhaps the 19-foot length was necessary.

The present owner reports that he rows *Blue Bill* frequently during the pleasant early morning hours along Grenadier and Tar islands when the river is very quiet. He also uses *Blue Bill* to teach his grandchildren the art of skiffing near the skiff's home port in Rockport, Ontario.

Blue Bill, *a 19-foot Canadian Dowsett St. Lawrence skiff, in front of the owner's summer home on Grenadier Island.*

The clean, attractive lines of the guideboat by L. E. Fry are evident in this wonderful 90-year-old classic.

L. E. Fry

A 1914 23.5-FOOT GUIDEBOAT

One of Clayton's better-known builders of fine launches was L. E. Fry. Interestingly enough, the Fry Boat Factory was located on the site now occupied by the Antique Boat Museum. This attractive, lightweight, 23.5-foot launch is constructed much like a carvel skiff, with white cedar planking, steam-bent oak ribs and a short mahogany deck. The 25-horsepower Gray Scout engine is her original power plant, providing modest speed and excellent maneuverability. Standard equipment also included a pair of copper-tipped spruce oars. The oars were a welcome feature for quietly securing the perfect location for fishing and hunting without having to start the noisy engine. This delightful launch has spent her entire life in the Thousand Islands and is currently based in the boathouse at the head of Comfort Island.

The attractive forward section of the carvel-planked cedar hull on the Fry guideboat presents a classic design that never grows old.

The stylish tumblehome and vee-transom show the design effort that went into this small guideboat.

Returning to her home port at the head of Comfort Island, the 1914 L. E. Fry guideboat is an excellent example of this important style.

Whisper

A 17-FOOT OLD TOWN CANOE

Whisper is a 40-year-old traditional wood-and-canvas canoe. She was a special model made by the Old Town Canoe Company in Maine, featuring rolled-back stems and wide gunwales. The wide gunwales provide additional strength so that the canoe can retain its shape without the need for thwarts. This feature gives the canoe the advantage of more useable room in the middle of the hull. The rolled-back stems give the canoe a very attractive appearance and add to its ability to handle choppy water effectively. This special canoe model was called the Molitor and was the most expensive model that Old Town offered.

Whisper was built in 1965 at the request of one of Old Town Canoe's dealers as a special gift for his wife. Its additional features included a complete 80-square-foot sailing rig, a sliding rowing seat with 7-foot spoon-bill oars for sculling, additional half ribs for extra stiffness, the special two-color paint option and varnished outside stems. It was intended to be a canoe with every option that Old Town offered, to provide a full range of canoe possibilities for the owner's entire family.

This versatile boat is frequently observed being rowed as a single scull with the rowing seat in the morning, sailed with her lateen sail during the afternoon, and paddled slowly along the shore in the evening. Her home port is on Cherry Island.

The versatile Old Town canoe Whisper *is ready for a brisk row around the islands as she assumes her alternate mode as a single scull.*

At left: *A closer look at the removable rowing seat that quickly converts a conventional canoe to a single scull for high-performance rowing.*

At right: *The forward seat in* Whisper *shows the opening for the mast between the spoon-bill oars that are used with the sliding rowing seat.*

Looking from the bow, the graceful curve of Anna's 18-foot shear is clearly evident.

Anna

AN 1895 ST. LAWRENCE SKIFF

The firm of Wilbur & Wheelock of Clayton, New York, was one of the premier St. Lawrence skiff builders of their time. Many of their skiffs have survived and are prized by their owners, who still regularly row them for exercise or fishing. Wilbur & Wheelock skiffs are also considered quite collectable for their fine detailing and the selection of woods used in their construction.

Built in 1895, *Anna* is the 18-foot model of the St. Lawrence skiff described in their catalog as having a 42-inch beam and a total weight of 120 pounds. The lapstrake beveled planking is clear white cedar, fastened with copper clinch nails. The gunwales and the decks are selected native walnut. The closely spaced steam-bent ribs are oak. The two rowing seats are white-pine-edged in walnut, with fan-shaped seats at the ends fitted with wicker seatbacks.

The 18-foot length was the most popular size among rowing skiffs, providing excellent capacity with ease of rowing and compact turning qualities. A good portion of *Anna's* life was spent in the Adirondacks before returning to the Thousand Islands more than 20 years ago. Her current home port is Comfort Island.

A simple eye strap mounted to the stem is ideal for mooring or towing the skiff properly.

The name plate of a well-respected St. Lawrence skiff builder.

The thole pin for oars facilitated netting fish without entanglement.

Harm

A 1936 23-Foot Cupernall Fishing Launch

Charles Cupernall and the Cupernall family built their boats in the cottage community of Thousand Island Park on Wellesley Island. They built skiffs, power launches and custom-designed boats for special customers. In 1922 Ira Cupernall built one of the family's most significant boats, the 35-foot racing launch *Miss St. Lawrence*, for Dr. George Stephens. Ira also built *School's Out II*, which is on exhibit at Harrah's Museum in Reno.

In 1936 Charles Cupernall built *Harm* on speculation and the following season sold it to a family at the head of Round Island as their primary fishing launch. The name *Harm* was the result of using the first letter of each family member's first name. The hull is

made entirely of cedar, with planking that is feather-edged. She is relatively lightweight and built for swift performance with modest power. In many ways *Harm* possesses many of the qualities of a St. Lawrence skiff and is ideally suited for fishing.

The family decided to donate *Harm* to the Antique Boat Museum in 1972. She was part of the collection for 25 years, when she was deaccessioned and offered back to her original family. Back at Round Island once more, she was fully restored and is very active on the river. A regular participant in boat shows, she's a frequent prizewinner.

This full side view of Harm *show the classic lines of the guide boat, which remained virtually unchanged for decades.*

This view of the Cupernall guideboat shows the roomy, open interior so well-suited for fishing and hunting.

Harm's vintage-style hull handles speed quite well considering it was designed for less power.

The boatbuilders at Duke Motor Service designed the Playmate model as an advanced version of their popular Dispro model.

The Duke Playmate

A 1954 17-FOOT DUKE PLAYMATE

Duke Marine Limited of Port Carling, Ontario, built a wide range of specialty boats that were favorites among the boaters of the Muskoka Lakes region. In 1924 Charlie Duke and Ernie Greavette were partners operating under the business name Duke & Greavette. Unfortunately, however, the company was unable to survive, and the partnership dissolved. Charlie Duke continued to work alone until his two sons were able to join him. Together they formed a new firm called Duke Motor Service. By the late 1920s boatbuilding was expanding rapidly, and the Dukes were fully occupied building motor launches.

In 1933 one of the Dukes' regular customers requested that they build a fishing boat that would be similar to the Disappearing Propeller Boats that were so popular in the region. But there were several differences that he wanted incorporated in the boat. He wanted it to have more beam, with a conventional transom, and for power he wanted a 15-horsepower Buchannan Baby Four. The Buchannan engines were manufactured in Orillia, Ontario, not too far away from the Duke boatbuilding facility. The new boat was so thoughtfully designed and built by the Dukes that the result fit their customer's needs perfectly, and other customers who saw the special model wanted one just like it. The Dukes knew that the new boat was something special, and it turned out to be one of their most enduring models.

The Dukes gave the new series the name Playmate. The boats were produced from 1933 until 1955 and every year made up a significant share of their total production. In a good year, the Duke craftsmen could build as many as twelve standardized Playmates, while still building a number of their custom models, which were always considered very special. The Playmate became a popular sport boat that was an ideal choice for lake fishing. The standard power became the 25-horsepower Buchannan Midget engine.

This 17-foot Playmate has been well maintained and is very true to the way she was received in 1954. She is an unpretentious, efficient boat that is ideal for the no-nonsense sportsman. She's also one of the last Playmates built, as the Dukes' main activity gradually evolved to full-time refinishing and restoration of the numerous wood boats in the region. In 1977 Duke Marine was sold but continued as the last one of the many original boatbuilders in the region. The home port for this attractive 1954 17-foot Duke Playmate is Comfort Island, near Alexandria Bay.

The Duke Playmate is an ideal small powerboat that is well suited for fishing in the protected waters of the Thousand Islands.

Sport Boats and Runabouts

One of the most interesting aspects of living on an island is the confirmation that first-time visitors will eventually seek. After looking all around the island and studying the view of the river from every angle, they begin to understand the special nature of island living — that a boat is not just another form of recreation; it's the only practical way to reach the mainland. Simply put, a boat is a necessity.

The term "Thousand Islands" sounds like an exaggeration, when in fact it's an understatement. There are more than 1,800 islands in the first 50 miles of the St. Lawrence River, creating a boater's wonderland of secluded passages, beautiful bays and welcoming harbors. This provides exactly the environment that recreational boaters enjoy most, and islanders love the fact that their boats are a mainstay of everyday living — that boating is an essential activity.

Islanders usually have several boats, each to serve a different purpose. It was in the early part of the nineteenth century, when the gasoline marine engine became the adopted power plant, that traveling to social gatherings on the islands became a popular activity. Swift little boats would run from one island to the next, dropping off their party-going passengers and earning the name "runabout."

Classic boaters identify a runabout as a decked-over craft with the driver and passenger seating located in cockpits. There can be one, two, three or even four cockpits in the runabout style, and the engine is somewhat hidden under a pair of deck hatches. From the 1920s through the 1950s, runabouts were very popular craft because of their overall speed and usually attractive styling.

The Century Viking How Jude *as seen from the aft cockpit of* Friendship, *a 30-foot Chris-Craft express cruiser.*

In the islands, where boating was a multi-faceted activity, there were other craft referred to as "sport boats" that were equally as popular. The launch was so popular on the river because its passengers occupied a large open area behind the driver, providing a better opportunity for conversation and socializing. It also allowed a folding convertible top to be conveniently carried just aft of the seating area in case the weather suddenly changed. The power plant in the launch was located forward of the driver, beneath a pair of deck hatches. The launch is generally classified as a displacement hull that provides a very comfortable, level ride that is quite pleasant for passengers and still capable of good speed.

During the Depression years, boat design changed a bit to focus on the more practical aspects of boating. The result of this new approach was the development of the style known as the "utility" boat. In many ways it was a very plain version of the runabout, nearly all open rather than decked over. The modest-sized engine was covered with a box in the center of a large open area. It was a useful boat, ideal for carrying passengers or supplies, or for fishing or water sports, and it fit the needs of many islanders and fishing guides perfectly. Local boatbuilders became adept at building the utility style with many custom features. The Thousand Islands boatbuilders certainly produced many beautiful custom runabouts; however, their greatest contribution was probably the transformation of the multi-purpose utility into an attractive sport boat that every self-respecting islander hoped to own one day.

Messenger, *a powerful and luxurious 28-foot Gar Wood runabout.*

Ol' Boy

A 1938 24-FOOT CHRIS-CRAFT SPORTSMAN

As the world emerged from the Great Depression following the 1929 stock-market crash, the surviving boatbuilders were doing everything they could to remain in business, including developing small, multi-purpose utility boats that were a bit more practical and had broader applications than sleek, expensive runabouts. "Utility" was appropriate for these rather plain and modest craft, but for promotion-conscious Chris-Craft, the term seemed to possess very little excitement.

By 1938, with recovery well on its way, Chris-Craft was ready to introduce a very special utility model that elevated the status of the craft to the more elite status enjoyed by runabout models. It would possess all of the practical features important to the utility models, along with the attractive styling normally associated with runabouts, including leather seating. What the new boat needed was a model name that would clearly put it ahead of all the other utilities. Chris-Craft decided to call it the Sportsman, and it would be announced as the featured boat in Chris-Craft's exhibit at the 1938 National Motor Boat Show.

A businessman from Utica, New York, who was also an ardent Thousand Islands fisherman, traveled to the 1938 National Motor Boat Show with his son to consider the possibility of upgrading from their 21-foot utility to a slightly larger craft. His summer home was

The transom view of Ol' Boy shows how its generous beam carried all the way aft.

49

The twin chrome-plated deck horns were standard features on the very special 24-foot Sportsman in 1938.

The Sportsman's modern windshield had sporty side wings and was protected by a full metal frame appropriate to the utility style.

The multi-instrument dashboard, the banjo-style steering wheel and the turquoise leather upholstery were among the Sportsman's attractive details.

just downriver from Alexandria Bay, on Dingman Point, and fishing was serious sport for him. He often traveled to several locations on the river with friends and his favorite guide, looking forward to their usual bountiful catch.

His first destination at the New York show was the Chris-Craft exhibit, where the new 24-foot Sportsman was featured. As soon as he observed the Sportsman, he knew immediately that this was the boat he wanted for the islands. It was incredibly handsome and yet perfectly suited for long fishing excursions.

As luck would have it, his local dealer from the Utica Boat Company was there at the same time, working his scheduled shift with the Chris-Craft sales personnel. The businessman and his son wanted the very same boat that was on display, and it took just a few minutes to put the deal together. The arrangements called for the boat to remain in New York until spring. The businessman's son would then return to New York by train and drive the boat to the Thousand Islands via the Hudson River to Troy, where he would travel on the Barge Canal and the Oswego Canal to Lake Ontario. From Oswego he would cross Lake Ontario to the St. Lawrence River. The trip would require traveling nearly 400 miles in order to reach their boathouse on Dingman Point. The businessman's son and a close friend made the trip in three days without a single problem. The family decided to honor their father's new boat by affectionately naming it *Ol' Boy*.

Three years later, the young man would enter the United States Navy to command a military craft with distinction in the Pacific Ocean during the most challenging period of the Second World War. The skills learned during his years of boating in the Thousand Islands served him well in the Pacific. And on Dingman Point in the Thousand Islands, the 24-foot Sportsman named *Ol' Boy* continues to serve the boating needs of that same family.

The attractive lines of the first Chris-Craft Sportsman set a new standard for sport-utilities in the Second World War era.

The view from the aft cockpit in a big runabout is a special treat never to be passed up.

Swiftwater

A 25-FOOT HACKER-DESIGNED HUTCHINSON RUNABOUT

By the 1920s the Hutchinsons established themselves as one of America's finest builders of mid-size, custom-designed boats. Their strength was well known in the design and construction of displacement launches, utilities and commuters. However, by 1930 a few of their regular customers expressed growing interest in having them build a special runabout model similar to those designed by John Hacker. Hacker was one of the most respected designers of runabouts and had often been commissioned by neighboring boatbuilder, Fitzgerald and Lee, to create their special runabouts and express cruisers. Hutchinson

decided to respond to this new interest and build a few runabouts with the special features that they preferred. He had Hacker prepare designs for three models, from 24 feet to 30 feet in length, with tasteful features that would suit the conditions normally expected on the river.

After building a few of the runabouts, interest slowed a bit. Then in 1937 a few interested customers asked Hutchinson once more to produce the 25-foot model. Between 1937 and 1938 Hutchinson built six of these special runabouts with carefully matched Honduras mahogany. The hulls were nearly identical, with each finished

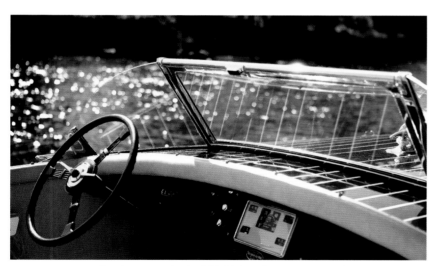

The three-panel windshield is a clear giveaway of John Hacker's design influence on this fine runabout.

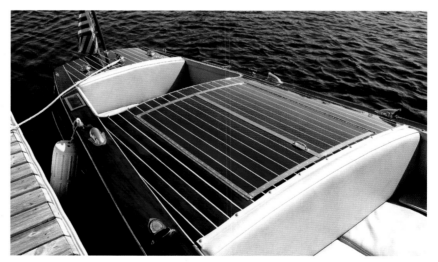

The midships and aft cockpit are roomy and comfortable.

*The influence of John Hacker is immediately evident
in the Hutchinson runabout* Swiftwater.

according to the owner's wishes. It was completed in 1938 as a present for young Anita Hagan, whose parents had their summer home on Ina Island. The Hagans requested that the forward double cockpit be arranged with a walk-through opening in the front seat. This simple change provided much easier access and movement for both the passengers and the operator. The boat was originally named *Shoal Shagger* before it was sold to Dorothy Weymss of Morgan Island, who renamed the boat *Wey Sassy*.

Although it was a runabout, the modified forward cockpits made it possible for Dorothy to use the boat for her frequent fishing trips, and she often used the boat daily on the river. After operating *Wey Sassy* for more than 40 years in the islands, Dorothy sold the boat to her friend Jim Lewis in 1983. Both families had been successfully involved in the paper business in northern New York. The boat was renamed *Swiftwater*, for a location close to where Jim Lewis grew up on the river. It was one of the first classic boats that Jim Lewis, a major benefactor to the Antique Boat Museum, had restored. The work was accomplished superbly, and the hull was stained a very dark shade of mahogany.

Lewis was the nephew of Grace Cornwall, whose summer home for many years was on Cuba Island. In 1989 Lewis sold *Swiftwater* to the present owner of Cuba Island, who said that the unique cockpit arrangement requested by the original owner in 1938 was a major factor in his purchase. *Swiftwater* continues to reside on Cuba Island and remains in superb operating condition.

At right: *This view from overhead shows* Swiftwater's *larger middle cockpit and walk-through front seat.*

How Jude

Like their pals at Chris-Craft, the Century Boat Company was well aware of the exclusivity that Lyman enjoyed as the principle source of Clinker-built lapstrake sea skiffs. Both Chris-Craft and Century made their reputations by building hard-chine, V-bottom, level-riding, fast boats. But by the early 1950s they could no longer ignore the ever-increasing share of the market that Lyman seemed to have to themselves. Chris-Craft's answer was to open a new Sea Skiff Division. Century responded by introducing its new Viking line of Clinker-built boats, and the competition was red hot by the mid-1950s.

The owners of this particular 19-foot Viking had a cottage on Downie Island and purchased it as their commuter to and from the Canadian mainland at Williams Marine Service. The original power was a 60-horsepower Gray Marine engine that would provide a top speed of 31 mph. It was just barely enough speed to allow the owner's two sons to use the Viking for water-skiing. They eventually convinced their father to re-power the boat with a 140-horsepower Volvo engine. The new engine was good for water-skiing, but excessively rough use at speed began to take its toll on the Viking hull, causing considerable leakage. Offered for sale, the marina

The attractive foredeck of the Century Viking.

How Jude's interior layout is perfect for fishing.

This view of How Jude *shows its large cockpit layout.*

At left: *The 19-foot Viking was a bold attempt by Century in the mid-1950s to capture a portion of the market dominated by Lyman.*

Touché

A 28-FOOT CHRIS-CRAFT SEA SKIFF

*The side steering station in the 19-foot Century Viking
is virtually identical to the arrangement in Lyman's famous Islanders.*

owner's son decided to purchase the boat, as he was sure that he could successfully repair it.

When the repairs were completed, the Volvo engine was reinstalled and the boat's integrity secured once again. After many years of reliable service, the Viking was purchased again by the owner's father in 1986. It was intended as a Christmas gift for his wife and finally named *How Jude*. After 13 years of pleasure, however, it was time for some serious repairs, including replacement of the Volvo with the original 60-horsepower Gray Marine engine. The work was finished in time to trailer the Viking to Florida for the 2004 Mt. Dora Boat Show and the popular 210-mile St. Johns River Cruise. In May the owners traveled to Manistee, Michigan, to participate in the Century Boat Show at the site where she was built in 1956.

In 1964 Chris-Craft's Sea Skiff Division presented the boating world with a superb 28-foot open model with the beam to provide the most abundant cockpit in its class. Under the broad forward deck was a spacious cuddy, with V-berths, a marine head and storage lockers. The prominent metal-framed ventilating windshields were angled back smartly to provide one of the most attractive sea skiff styles offered by any builder. All of this and its powerful 275-horsepower V-8 engine made the 28-foot sea skiff a leader in its field and a choice for every serious sportsman to carefully consider.

In the Thousand Islands, fishing guides found this model to be an ideal size for large groups when traveling longer distances in choppy seas. For nearly 30 seasons in the islands *Touché* was the flagship of one of the area's most successful professional fishing guides. By the time he finally retired from active guiding, his boat was ready for a more gentle approach to boating. She had been worked hard for many years and needed someone to give her the attention necessary to look her best once more. The new owners loved all the room she offered, as well as the marvelous styling. They had the time and the interest to return this attractive sea skiff to her original condition. After three decades of constant, hard service as a guide's boat, many areas required attention and repair. The new owners developed a systematic restoration plan, facing one problem at a time while still regularly using the boat.

Today, her owners frequently cruise to Clayton, Morristown, Rockport, Gananoque, Kingston and other locations for dinner or to

A fine example of the husky hull on Chris-Craft's 28-foot sea skiff, and the reason why it remains so popular among professional fishing guides.

meet friends. She is a roomy, comfortable, open sport boat capable of excellent speed and able to handle rough seas superbly. The full width of the hull is carried all the way to the transom, giving the boat an exceptionally spacious, deep cockpit for an open 28-foot boat. This sea skiff hull was also perfectly suited to its adaptation as the hull for Chris-Craft's popular 28-foot sea skiff express cruiser. It is one of Chris-Craft's best designs, and it has been worked as hard as any boat during its 40 years on the river.

This aft view of Touché *provides some idea of the extreme beam that goes right to the transom on these Chris-Craft sea skiffs.*

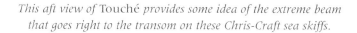

The 26-foot Lyman utility is one of the most popular designs among Thousand Islanders.

Belacqua

The Lyman Boat Company of Sandusky, Ohio, took great pride in the soft-riding qualities that their beamy lapstrake hull provided in the choppy conditions common to Lake Erie. Lyman owners who enjoyed the smooth performance provided by the well-designed hull were steadfast in their loyalty to Lyman, as they moved up to larger models when required. (Even the giant builder Chris-Craft was so impressed with the growing popularity of lapstrake hulls that they opened a totally new Sea Skiff Division to produce round-bilge lapstrake boats in the mid-1950s.)

Belacqua was originally delivered to the New Jersey coast, where the lapstrake hull configuration was quite popular. Along the Jersey shore, where offshore fishing was very popular, there were a number of regional builders using this construction style. *Belacqua's* next owner brought her to Cos Cob, Connecticut, where she continued her service in saltwater. Her wood hull seemed to benefit from the "pickling effect" of salt. The new owner is convinced of the benefits gained by early exposure to saltwater when he declares that his 40-year-old hull is 100-percent original and solid as a rock.

In these views of Belacqua, *the generous flare of her hull, which makes her so seaworthy in choppy seas, is quite apparent.*

The generous beam of the 26-foot Lyman provides excellent interior room all the way to the transom, allowing a large number of passengers.

The name *Belacqua* was selected during a time when the owner's wife was deeply emerged in the study of Italian literature. The focal point of her studies was the writing of Dante and one of his principal characters, Belacqua. The name remains because it has a rhythmic flow and seems to fit the boat's personality so well.

Lyman refers to this model as the Sleeper because it is equipped with standard V-bunks in the cuddy cabin. The 26-foot model was one of Lyman's most popular hull lengths and carries a beam of more than 9 feet, with a generous cockpit depth of more than 3 feet from floor to rail. The hull gains its full width close to the stem and carries its width nearly all the way to the transom, creating a very roomy and comfortable cockpit. The hull is Clinker-built, with five-ply fir plywood overlapping planking over steam-bent white oak frames.

Belacqua is an everyday boat that is ideal for commuting, taking loads of passengers to church on Sundays, or all-day fishing trips. She is fast enough for tubing or water-skiing and ideal for a quiet cruise among the islands. If an island family were limited to just one boat, the 26-foot Lyman would be a perfect choice.

Royal Lady

A 1948 26-Foot Hutchinson Sport-Utility

Hutchinson's post–Second World War sport-utilities were thought by many to be the ultimate boat for the river sportsman. The skilled hand of Glen Furness, Hutchinson's in-house naval architect, implemented just enough changes to lift this standard model to a level of modern styling that would appeal to upscale post-war expectations.

The upper portion of the stem was attractively rounded to flow with the curve of the covering boards. The beautiful three-sectioned mahogany windshield was attractively angled to provide a classic modern look, the oversize side wings serving to support a cleverly designed top that was easily removed when not in use. The center section of the windshield could be lifted for perfect ventilation or quickly removed for easy access to adjust the anchor line. The hull's beam was increased and moved well forward to increase the flare and make the boat drier in rough seas. Perhaps the most innovative feature, however, and often unnoticed, was the hard chine built into the traditional round hull. This creative idea provided resistance to rolling, helped the hull plane and didn't diminish the traditional soft ride in choppy seas.

In this view of the 26-foot Hutchinson Royal Lady, *it is easy to observe her classic features and understand why she is so highly respected among classic boaters.*

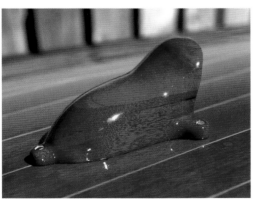

Clockwise from left:

The hand-carved air scoops were a craftsman's gift
to the previous owner of Royal Lady.

The windshield frame supports are another example
of Hutchinson's craftsmanship.

The large side frames connect to the windshield support
bows allowing for an ingenious stow-away canvas top.

This custom wood steering wheel was added later.

With her large V-8 and innovative bottom design, Royal Lady *is capable of high-speed performance.*

This was a boat that was extremely comfortable, beautifully constructed with select mahoganies, fast, and as attractive as any post-war sport-utility; however, it was expensive to build, so production was limited to four or five boats each year.

Royal Lady spent several seasons on Cherry Island as *Win Lee* before moving to Round Island, her present home port. Her owners have always provided wonderful care, and her immaculate appearance is evidence of thoughtful ownership over six decades.

It was 30 years ago that one of the refinishers from Hutchinson's was so taken with this magnificent boat that he fashioned four mahogany air scoops, shaped exactly like the original metal ones, to present to the owner as a possible alternative. The response was positive, and they have become one of the boat's unique features, along with its vintage mahogany steering wheel. *Royal Lady* remains one of the best examples of the Hutchinson 26-foot post-war sport-utility model and is frequently observed touring the islands.

The Gar Wood runabout Zipalong *cruises past her Thousand Islands home, Bella Vista.*

Zipalong

I n 1936 Gar Wood introduced a new 18-foot twin-cockpit runabout, with both cockpits located forward of the engine rather than one cockpit forward and one aft of the engine. This arrangement was unusual for a small runabout and introduced a new era in the design of these craft. One of the most productive dealers for Gar Wood boats was Fitzgerald & Lee, located in Alexandria Bay, where year after year they were among the company's volume sales leaders.

The nifty little runabout was originally delivered to its first owner in Philadelphia before working its way north to the Thousand Islands. She arrived without any name, and one of the first Thousand Islands owners decided to search the boat register of the Chippewa Bay Yacht Club for a suitable name from the past. The old boats were listed alphabetically by their given names, and nothing seemed to fit until they got to the very last entry, and there it was — *Zipalong*. It was the perfect name to describe the special qualities of this small, highly maneuverable sport boat.

Gar Wood runabouts have a long, rich heritage in the Thousand Islands. One of the most famous is the 33-foot Baby Gar known as *Snail*. In 1926 Edward Noble purchased *Snail*. The boat was powered with a single Liberty aircraft engine that developed 500 horsepower and achieved speeds above 50 mph. It was so fast that legend in the islands has it that the owner guaranteed a standing offer of $1,000 to anyone could beat him in a race. The offer stood for years, and no one was ever known to beat *Snail* in a race. She is one of the treasured boats of the Thousands Islands and is permanently exhibited in the Antique Boat Museum in Clayton.

The 18-foot Gar Wood runabout presented a very well-proportioned, modern sport boat for 1936 and remains one of the classic designs.

At high speed, Zipalong is a level-riding runabout that packs thrilling performance into its 18 feet of length.

This view shows the tumblehome styling at the transom, the forerunner to the barrel backs that appeared a few years later.

The handsome dashboard in this 1936 Gar Wood runabout.

Corker

A 1939 19-Foot Hutchinson

Nineteen feet was an unusual size for a Hutchinson standardized model. There were only three similar boats of this length built during this era, making *Corker* a very rare craft. She was built for the Collins family of Jug Island in 1939, and they simply named her *Jug*. After some 20 years of service on Jug Island, she was offered for sale to the owner of an Alexandria Bay supply store. When he saw the boat for the first time he said to his son, "Isn't she a corker?" and the name stuck.

Corker has been in regular service to the same family for 40 years. She's used for fishing, commuting and touring. The walk-through passage between the two front seats is a standard Hutchinson feature

Corker has excellent speed, good maneuverability and a strong hull, well suited to the conditions in the Thousand Islands.

that allows easier movement to facilitate docking, tending to fenders and fishing. The anchor horn on the bow has been standard equipment for serious fishing on the river for decades. It permits easy location changes for your boat in the right spot to get the day's catch. The mahogany-frame windshield was added to accommodate the addition of a folding canvas top several years ago. Although the wood-frame windshield was not original to the boat, it is an accurate duplicate of the same style used by Hutchinson.

Corker has been re-powered and has had a few bottom planks replaced over the years. Her regular boathouse is still located at the supply store on Otter Creek, in Alexandria Bay. Her copper-riveted lapstrake Honduras mahogany hull has been maintained beautifully. Her topsides planks are the full length of the hull, bookmatched with no butt joints. Her sharp entry forward assures a soft ride in the choppy water that is common in the busy harbor area in which she usually operates.

Traditional mahogany fishing-rod holders mounted to the ceiling boards in a Hutchinson utility.

The classic Thousand Islands anchor horn was virtually standard equipment on every Hutchinson utility if fishing was a consideration.

Corker has spent nearly 70 years in the Thousand Islands.

Looking from the stern quarter, the open style of this guideboat is very similar to the typical utility.

Times A Wastin'

There are so many stories related to the former boatbuilding days in Alexandria Bay that it's sometimes difficult to separate truth from fiction; however, most summer residents tend to believe most of the stories told, because over time they're repeated so often. This story is similar to the legend about the GI who was stationed overseas. Each week while he was in the Army he would mail home one small part from a jeep. After being discharged and returning home, he opened the packages, assembled the parts, and had a fully-functional jeep.

There are some boats in the Thousand Islands that look very much like Hutchinson boats, but they're not Hutchinsons. The manufacturer's name listed on the registration is the name of the individual who built the boat, who in many cases was also a boat carpenter who worked at Hutchinson. It seems, as the story goes, that it was common practice at the end of the day for a worker to take home a discarded plank or a rib that didn't quite fit, or any miss-cut board. Over a period of several months these scraps of wood began to take on the shape of a boat in the worker's garage.

The foredeck on Times A Wastin' *with the lifting eye, the power winch and the anchor horn, all essential items for Thousand Islands guides.*

Traditional fishing guides often preferred their boats to be equipped with the more efficient stick-steering system.

Although it's a no-nonsense guideboat, the 1948 Dingman had a few features that set it apart,
such as rounded covering boards, a modern stem profile and a raked transom.

It was in the spring of 1948 that a boat named *Times A Wastin'* emerged from one of these garages.

Times A Wastin' is an original riverboat built by a local craftsman primarily for fishing. The seating arrangement and the placement of the controls and gauges are well suited to fishing. The traditional stick-steering system is responsive and convenient. Most of the local home-built boats have painted hulls. The reason for painting the hulls may have been that the surplus planks were blemished or mismatched in terms of color and grain patterns. The importance of this boat is her genuine character and her no-nonsense approach to the intended role she was built to fulfill. She is virtually unchanged from the day she was launched nearly 60 years ago and has spent her whole life in the bay area. In many ways this boat and her name accurately represent traditional river culture.

The Ark

A 1915 26-Foot L. E. Fry Launch

There is a distinct possibility that this attractive Fry launch has been in the same family for more than 90 years. The current owner's great-grandfather previously owned the same cottage that his family purchased in 1960. At the time of purchase, the 1915 Fry was included with the furnishings of the cottage, and there is good reason to believe that it had been there since the time the buyers great-grandfather owned the cottage.

The original Ford Model-T Clayton conversion marine engine was replaced some years ago with a more dependable Chris-Craft 4-cylinder Model-B engine. This engine seems to be an ideal replacement, providing good performance without undue weight and with enough speed for the younger family members to learn to water ski. In the 1960s the boat was the main source of water transportation for the island family on every trip to the mainland. She has been well maintained and still possesses nearly all of her original planking as she approaches her centennial year.

This photo clearly illustrates that the Fry launches followed the long-and-narrow design theme of the era.

At speed, The Ark's *displacement hull creates an enormous bow wave.*

The hatch-mounted vintage cowl ventilator.

A pair of wicker chairs was a regular adornment in nearly every launch's cockpit.

Fry's respected builder's plaque.

The long-deck displacement-hull launch enjoyed universal popularity before giving way in the 1920s to runabouts with planning hulls.

The Molly T is a classic long-deck launch built by Burch in 1918.

Molly T

A 1918 27-FOOT LAUNCH

The *Molly T* is a traditional-style displacement launch built in Ogdensburg, New York, in 1918. The builder's last name was Burch, and it's likely that he was associated with Joseph Leyare, who operated a very successful boatbuilding operation in Ogdensburg during that same time period. Leyare is best remembered as the builder of the well-known Thousand Islands one-design raceboats, or "numbers boats." The contract with Leyare specified that he was to build 20 identical boats to rigid specifications to participate in races. Burch was both a boatbuilder and fishing guide, and was probably employed by Leyare to help complete this sizeable contract. And like so many craftsmen of his time, he may have built boats at home after finishing his workday with Leyare.

The design and overall appearance of *Molly T* is typical of the launches of this era. Her hull sides and bottom were planked in white cedar, with the decks and transom of Honduras mahogany. Most of her planking is original, attesting to years of thoughtful care. She was re-powered with a Chrysler Marine 6-cylinder Ace engine in 1978 to provide reliable power for everyday operation. Although she has experienced several owners over the past 87 years, she has spent her entire life on the St. Lawrence River. Her current home port is Rockport, Ontario.

A pair of wicker chairs in the cockpit of the Molly T.

Molly T's *straightforward instrument panel.*

The traditional Thousand Islands anchor horn on the bow of the Molly T.

The Molly T *at her dock on Grenadier Island alongside her owners' Chris-Craft Capri.*

At left: *This interesting view of the* Molly T *provides a glimpse of her long, narrow hull, designed for speed.*

Canada Bird

A 1969 26-Foot Lyman Sleeper

One of the well-known restaurants for boaters in the Thousand Islands is a place called Foxy's, at Fishers Landing. Located right on the water's edge, it's a convenient place for boaters to tie up and be assured of having a good meal. One evening the owner of Foxy's was overheard saying to some friends that business was so good that he rarely had time to use his own 26-foot Lyman. When the present owner of *Canada Bird*, who was sitting close by, heard the conversation, he thought he should ask if the boat was for sale. It was, and together they went over to look at the boat. The Lyman was sitting on blocks with part of the bottom removed, and it was quickly apparent that it was a bit more than working at the

restaurant that kept the Lyman off the river. However, it didn't take long before the two reached a deal and the Lyman traveled across the border to Canada, where new bottom planks were installed and the entire boat restored to show-quality standards.

Re-powered with a 250-horsepower V-8 Crusader, the Lyman is an outstanding river boat capable of excellent speed and performance. It has the capacity to handle several passengers without disrupting its smooth ride or safety. The owners, who are islanders, have found this boat to be perfect for cruising, fishing, commuting and carrying supplies to their island in any kind of weather, even on choppy seas.

At speed, Mor-Joy is an impressive runabout, providing a comfortable and level ride.

Mor-Joy

A 1955 21-Foot Chris-Craft Capri Runabout

The original owner of this wonderful Chris-Craft Capri was the man who built Bonnie Castle Marina in Alexandria Bay. It was his special boat, which he enjoyed for eight years before selling it to the current owner. The Capri was in the refinishing shop at Bonnie Castle when the new owner saw her. He made the purchase of the boat as she was, had her launched, and after she sufficiently soaked-up, drove the unfinished Capri across the river to Rockport, Ontario, where Edward Huck completed the refinishing work at his marina. Since that time the boat has been refinished from the wood up and is considered one of the best examples of this popular Chris-Craft model in the Thousand Islands. She is a frequent entry in the regional classic boat shows and always draws lots of attention for her classic good looks and the impressive wraparound-style windshield.

Mor-Joy is still powered by her original Chris-Craft 158-horse-power 6-cylinder MBL engine, which provides power for speeds to 40 mph. Her substantial weight and deep forward entry help provide a comfortable ride in rough water conditions, making the 21-foot Capri one of Chris-Craft's most desirable post-war runabouts.

The convertible top for a double cockpit runabout like Mor-Joy *is a rare option that can be very important for island commuting.*

Some of the important styling features of Chris-Craft's Capri are the marvelous wraparound windshield and black alligator trim.

Night Rider, *one of the few surviving Thousand Islands one design raceboats, glides past the McNally houseboat,* La Duchesse.

Night Rider

A 28-FOOT THOUSAND ISLANDS ONE-DESIGN

Thousand Islanders enjoyed remarkable success in the early years of the Gold Cup races, winning the trophy for nine consecutive years. This remarkable series of victories stimulated members of the Thousand Islands Yacht Club to propose a plan for one-design racing in the Thousand Islands. The concept was to build a fleet of identical boats, powered with identical engines, where winning would be determined by the skill of the driver. The concept quickly won favor, and the design was prepared for a 28-foot launch known as the Thousand Islands One-Design. Nineteen brave members of the yacht club signed up to participate by each pledging to purchase one of the new raceboats. Joseph Leyare, in Ogdensburg,

New York, was selected to be the sole builder of the identical boats, since his local boatbuilding shop was the only one capable of producing an order this size by the following season.

The order was for 19 identical 28-foot launches with identical 30-horsepower, three-cylinder, two-cycle Jencick engines. The boats were designed to be dual purpose so that they could be used for general river transportation when not involved in races. In the summer of 1909 the entire fleet of 19 numbered boats was finished and delivered. The new boats and their owners were now ready to compete for a series of special trophies, in races that would create quite a bit of local interest.

A large, single-cowl vent is a common feature on most long-deck launches.

Night Rider's high-styled vee-transom with plenty of tumblehome was considered state-of-the-art in 1909.

The roomy cockpit makes it an ideal boat for taking guests on pleasant tours through the islands.

Night Rider's *level-riding displacement hull moves swiftly upriver as it passes under the Thousand Islands International Bridge.*

As the competition heated up during the course of the season, some of the owners felt that they needed to get a bit more power from their engines. They didn't hesitate to employ the best mechanics to make modifications in their quest to win. Modifications spread, however, and within a few years the one-design concept of identical boats was abandoned, marking the end of racing for the numbers boats.

Gradually, the original boats were modified to more adequately meet the boating needs of their owners for daily river transportation. *Night Rider* is one of the Thousand Islands one-design boats built by Leyare in 1909. She has been maintained beautifully and is often used for an evening cruise on the river. Occasionally *Night Rider* will participate in one of the local antique boat shows. When that happens, she always draws a crowd of onlookers who marvel at her introduction as a raceboat nearly a hundred years ago.

Built in 1882, Rock Island lighthouse still guides ships through the picturesque and dangerous American Narrows.

Night Rider's long, narrow hull was designed for speed. It still looks fast even while tied to her dock.

The Hutchinson launch C.D.S. alongside her home port on Estrellita Island.

C.D.S.

A 1914 30-FOOT HUTCHINSON BROTHERS LAUNCH

Though *C.D.S.* is sometimes mistaken for one of the original numbers boats, she was built just a few years after the famous racing fleet was delivered to Thousand Islands Yacht Club members. Her general appearance shows a strong resemblance to the Leyare design, with a long, narrow hull and high-crown mahogany deck. Most launches of this era, however, did appear remarkably similar, as regional builders seemed to stabilize around this attractive and comfortable style.

The boat was originally built for Judge Hasbrook, who spent his summers on Manhattan Island. After a few additional owners she was sold to a Dr. Birch, who also owned *G.L.R.*, a 40-foot Hutchinson commuter also known as the "Grand Lady of the River." She was sold from Dr. Birch's extensive boat collection to her present owner 35 years ago. At the time she was in dire need of serious restoration and was not really fit for use. She was wrapped in a huge sheet of polyethylene in order to float to her new home on Estrellita Island, where the restoration would take place.

The restoration was a complete success and eventually included a new Crusader V-6 engine to replace the former engine, a 1924 Chrysler. *C.D.S.* became the owner's personal launch and is used daily all summer. The name *C.D.S.* follows both a family tradition and the tradition among islanders of naming one important boat with the initials of her owner.

The level-riding C.D.S. *slices through the waves smoothly, providing excellent visibility for her helmsman.*

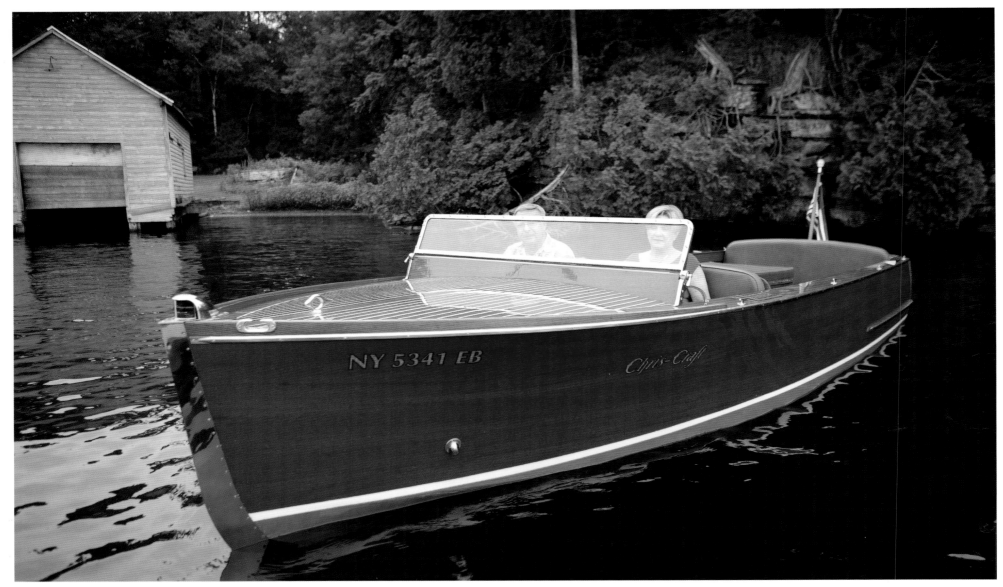

A wonderfully restored 1938 Chris-Craft utility, Aria *has been a frequent award-winner at the Clayton and Alexandria Bay Boat Shows.*

Aria

Marine historians claim the Great Depression that followed the 1929 stock market crash was the motivating force that resulted in the development of the basic utility boat. Utility boats were introduced as the bare-bones, "plain Jane" of boats. They were priced so low that there was virtually no margin for profit. Their role for boatbuilders was to keep up some level of production during a dreadful economic period; however, by the mid-1930s the utility concept was starting to catch on with boaters, and gradually the models became more attractive. By the late 1930s the utility model had clearly become a better looking boat, and *Aria* is a wonderful example of how Chris-Craft was starting to elevate their utility models into attractive, comfortable sport boats for a rapidly expanding market.

The small, multi-purpose utility boat was well suited to the variety of activities offered in the Thousand Islands. It was a perfect style for summer residents and islanders who were always using their boats to move cargo, take advantage of the abundant fishing, or simply tour the river with guests. Chris-Craft realized the potential of the utility design and felt that the boat needed an appealing model name. Their answer was to identify it as their "Sportsman" model. The 21-foot utility became the 22-foot Sportsman and would become their all-time production volume leader.

The walk-through front seat
has been a welcome standard feature on Chris-Craft utilities for decades.

Aria moves cleanly through the river at low speed.

Mercer's Shipyard in Clayton was the Thousand Islands Chris-Craft dealer that delivered this 21-foot utility to the Sims family at their Lake of the Isles cottage in 1938. After nearly 50 seasons of pleasure in the Thousand Islands, the family decided to donate their Chris-Craft to the Antique Boat Museum. However, a few years later the museum decided that it would require too much work to get the boat ready for exhibit, and reluctantly decided it would be better to deaccession it.

The high bidder on the boat asked the museum to recommend a restorer who could return the boat to its original condition. The new owner met with the restorer to develop a plan to bring the boat as close to its original condition as possible. After a winter's work the job was finished in the spring of 1991. The new owners were delighted with the transformation. They were also opera-lovers and decided to name their boat *Aria,* since arias are solo in nature and she was one-of-a-kind in their eyes.

They were so pleased with the results that they would use any excuse to take friends on tours through the islands aboard *Aria.* They also decided that besides using the boat for pure enjoyment, they should enter her in a few classic boat shows. It is no surprise that she has been awarded numerous trophies, including Best Antique Utility in 1995 and 1999 at the prestigious Clayton Boat Show.

1949 Lyman

A 1949 13.5-Foot Lyman Outboard Runabout

The present owner's uncle purchased this standard Lyman outboard runabout during the summer of 1949 in Alexandria Bay from Van's Marine. It was originally powered by one of the new 10-horsepower Mercury motors that were becoming well known for their strong performance. In 1957 the owner decided that the Lyman would make a splendid gift for his 12-year-old nephew, who also spent summers in the Thousand Islands and had always admired the boat.

Years later, when the nephew's daughter was 12, she was given custody of the Lyman as her personal boat. By this time the boat was powered by an 18-horsepower Johnson. She operated the Lyman for several years, learning the responsibility of operating a small boat prudently on a major international waterway. Then, after a pleasurable time with the Lyman, she moved on to another boat.

The Lyman is still in the same family and used frequently. She has always enjoyed having a slip inside the family's Wellesley Island boathouse. And though a few cracked ribs have been replaced, she has never required extensive restoration and still has all of her original plywood planking. She waits, available and ready, for the next young boater in the family to learn the skills and responsibility of boating in the Thousand Islands.

*The 13-foot Lyman runabout
has the full-width passenger seat located in front of the helm.*

*The helm is just behind the passenger seat and ideally located
to keep everything clean and simple in this practical boat.*

At operating speed, Messenger *presents itself as an attractive, level-riding classic.*

Messenger

A 1929 28-Foot Gar Wood Baby Gar Runabout

The year 1929 was remarkably good for boatbuilders. Nearly every builder was working to capacity, and their boats were selling faster than they could build them — the 1929 National Motor Boat Show set new sales records for every major builder. Many builders, including Chris-Craft, Dodge and Gar Wood, immediately prepared expansion plans to build new factories, unaware of the impending economic disaster.

Gar Wood's most popular model for 1929 was their new flush-deck 28-foot Baby Gar runabout, which was offered as an open model or a limousine. With three plush cockpits and speeds to 40 mph, the 28-foot Baby Gar was every sportsman's dream. One of Gar

The 28-foot triple-cockpit Gar Wood runabout was the most popular model in their entire fleet up to the start of the Second World War.

Messenger's neat instrument panel is harmonious with the straightforward design of this runabout.

A popular option on large Gar Wood runabouts was the "one-man" folding top, so named because one person could easily raise or lower it when the weather changed.

Messenger's clean, classic lines are evident as she idles down to return to her home port.

Wood's most productive dealers worldwide was Fitzgerald & Lee, located in Alexandria Bay, where *Messenger* was delivered to G. W. Benson in mid-summer of that year.

All four of *Messenger*'s successive owners have been Thousand Islanders. The only other Gar Wood with more tenure in the Thousand Islands than *Messenger* is *Snail*, the famous 1926 33-foot Baby Gar owned by E. J. Noble. *Snail* is one of just six remaining 33-foot Baby Gars, and she is part of the permanent collection of the Antique Boat Museum. *Messenger* has been re-powered with a V-8 Crusader and continues to be very active on the river, often sporting her original one-man convertible top. She is a frequent participant in local classic boat shows, often taking top honors in her class.

Lo'Fin'Too *presents an attractive impression at speed, showing the positive forward lift of Lyman's hull in a choppy sea.*

Lo'Fin'Too

The 19-foot Lyman inboard runabout model was built from 1957 through 1960. *Lo'Fin'Too* was built during the final year of production, shipped to the dealership in Clayton and then delivered to her owner on Wolfe Island, where she still resides. The 19-footer was the upgraded successor to the popular 18-foot runabout model, which was offered from 1955 through 1957. All together there were nearly 2,000 of the 18-and 19-foot runabouts built during this period, making it one of the most popular Lyman models offered.

Thirty-six years after *Lo'Fin'Too* was delivered to the Deming family of Wolfe Island, it was time for a complete restoration. A good friend of the family operated a boat restoration shop nearby on the island, so the job was given to the Wolfe Island Boat Shop, where new decks, a new transom and several hull planks were replaced. The family also decided it was time for more power, and a 130-horsepower engine was installed.

Everything looked so good that they decided on new upholstery and a new canvas top to complete the job, as a new generation of Demings continues to use *Lo'Fin'Too* regularly, keeping the boating tradition with their Lyman alive and well.

Lyman's tough lapstrake hull is well suited for smoothing out the choppy wave conditions often experienced on the St. Lawrence River.

The 30-foot open Sportsman with nearly 11 feet of beam has been called the zenith of Lyman hull designs representing years of improvements.

American Beauty

A 30-FOOT RESTYLED LYMAN SPORTSMAN

American Beauty was one of twelve 30-foot Sportsman models built by Lyman in 1969, the first year of production for this model. It is, in reality, the largest version of the legendary Lyman hull used for an open model. Sometimes from a distance it's difficult to determine the length of the Lyman being observed because they are designed so well that they are proportionately very similar. It's when the 30-footer is up close, or alongside one of Lyman's 26-footers, that its size becomes so apparent. The character of its superior

The Lyman 30-foot Sportsman is a marvelous craft for a wide range of travel through the Thousand Islands.

hull takes over in heavy seas, providing ample security and comfort. Some experts believe that it may be Lyman's finest hull in terms of overall performance.

Her original home port was Henderson Harbor, at the eastern end of Lake Ontario. The current owner purchased her in 1996 and brought her to his summer home near Cape Vincent. After a near sinking resulting from the deteriorated condition of the hull, major problems became painfully apparent. A decision was made to save the boat by performing a total restoration of the hull. But as work progressed, it became clear that the project was much greater than first imagined. The work was so extensive that the boat has often been classified as a "reproduction" by boat show officials because so much of it is new. Fortunately, the owner also operates a large, modern boat-restoration facility, where his team was able to reconstruct the boat and include many tasteful custom features that transformed a good design into a superb boat. As a result, the boat receives very special attention for its interesting improvements, improvements that often baffle boat show judges. However, the changes have made a very sweet boat even better, and whenever she enters a classic boat show, she comes out an award-winner, having even captured the highly coveted People's Choice Award.

American Beauty remains one of the great classic boats in the Thousand Islands and a treat to see. With her size and cuddy cabin, it's difficult not to consider *American Beauty* closer to a pocket cruiser than an open utility. She serves as a fine commuter and exceeds the speed of many runabouts.

The husky lapstrake hull of Black & Tan *is ideal for handling rough seas and large waves.*

Black & Tan

A 24-FOOT HUBERT JOHNSON SPORT BOAT

The Hubert Johnson Boat Works on the Jersey Shore was one of the early builders of fine lapstrake offshore sport-fishing boats. They were rugged, sea-kindly and extraordinarily handsome. Nearly all the Hubert Johnson boats left their plant with their hulls painted in the traditional black finish.

In 1951 the current owner's grandfather ordered the 24-foot sport model to use on Canandaigua Lake near Rochester, New York. The beefy hull provided a monumental wake that challenged all the children as they learned to water ski behind the big boat. Years later, after

the grandfather's death, the boat that had brought so much pleasure to the family was sold out of the family when the estate was settled.

Fifteen years passed. The granddaughter and her husband were now spending their summers in the Thousand Islands and began to yearn for the old Hubert Johnson sport boat from Canandaigua Lake. Unfortunately, they didn't have a clue where the old boat might be, and decided to simply look for something similar. A friend saw an interesting ad in *Wooden Boat* magazine and forwarded the information to them. They decided to have a look at the boat.

The remote-controlled brass spotlight, properly mounted on top of the windshield of Black & Tan, *is a good friend when returning to your island after dark.*

The deck-mounted powered windlass facilitates raising the anchor quickly to improve fishing locations.

The barn where the boat was stored was very dark, and the boat appeared dirty and in rough shape. However, it seemed to be rather similar in size and style to the old family boat. They returned for a second visit with a flashlight to examine the boat more carefully and look for any possible dry rot. In the small cuddy they found an old fishing hat, and inside the hat they discovered a plastic bag with an old registration. With the flashlight they could read the name, and to their amazement, it was the grandfather's registration. They had found his boat!

From there the boat was brought to one of the Thousand Islands restoration shops to be returned to its original splendor. A new, wider boathouse was built at their home at Westminster Park, on Wellesley Island, where the boat resides. After the restoration was completed the unnamed boat was christened *Black & Tan*, a name that fits her perfectly.

Above: Black & Tan*'s deck-mounted brass horn does the job and doesn't require much space. At left: The comfortable helm provides excellent visibility and a removable panel in the canvas top.*

Seen from the windows of the living quarters in her boathouse, Black & Tan *gets lined-up to enter the security of her slip below.*

Built in 1945, Elegant Lady *is one of the first Hackercraft runabouts produced after World War II
and also one of the last standardized triple-cockpit models from this legendary builder.*

Elegant Lady

A 26-FOOT HACKERCRAFT RUNABOUT

The runabouts designed by noted naval architect John Hacker are among the most sought-after of all sport boats. There was always something very special about the mystique connected with Hacker's runabouts — they were fast, they were innovative and they were different.

Elegant Lady was one of the first post–Second World War runabouts, built in early 1945. (Most of the major boatbuilding firms introduced their new production as 1946 models.) This 26-footer was shipped to Peoria, Illinois, where its first owner resided. The boat was used frequently, but in 1960 the original owner simply left her in an old barn, where she remained unattended for the next 18 years. At that time an old air force buddy of the present owner heard about the abandoned Hacker and wrote to him with a few details, encouraging a visit. After seeing the boat, a deal was struck, and the Hackercraft arrived at Fishers Landing a week later. It has been there ever since. After being rebuilt a few times, she was replaced with a 225-horsepower Crusader for greater dependability. She was restored in 1978 and has been maintained superbly ever since. *Elegant Lady* has been a regular winner at boat shows and is a popular boat on the river.

Some of the nice detailing at the aft cockpit on Elegant Lady.

Transoms were always given special attention in John Hacker's design studio.

One of the great old launches in the Thousand Islands, Monitor *cruises past its home port at Castle Rest on Pullman Island.*

Monitor

A 1906 38-Foot Hutchinson Launch

When George Pullman, wealthy manufacturer of the railroad sleeper car that bears his name, passed away in 1897, his island home, Castle Rest, remained in the family. Pullman's son-in-law was Frank Lowden, who took charge of the island home and contracted to have a 38-foot luxury launch built by the Hutchinson Brothers Boat Works in Alexandria Bay for the 1906 season. The launch-style craft features a displacement hull where the inboard engine is located just forward of midships. The large cockpit and helm are located just aft of the engine. This design style provides a smooth, level ride for passengers and a very stately appearance at all speeds. When the new launch was completed, Lowden named her *Monitor*.

The Lowden family enjoyed spending their summers at Castle Rest on Pullman Island and touring the river in their attractive

Like all displacement launches, Monitor *cuts the water cleanly, only slightly raising its bow.*

launch. Frank Lowden became a well-respected political leader in Chicago and in 1917 he was elected governor of the state of Illinois, serving until 1923. It was at about this time that the Hagans of Ina Island decided to construct a very large boathouse adjacent to their fabulous summer home. The upper floor of the new boathouse had a grand ballroom where the Hagans held formal dances during the summer season. The ballroom was larger than the dance floors that any of the large hotels along the river could provide.

In an act of great generosity, Governor and Mrs. Lowden presented the Hagans with their precious 38-foot *Monitor* as a special housewarming gift at the first dance held in the new boathouse and ballroom. It was an impressive way to commemorate the completion of the magnificent structure.

Monitor was one of the Hutchinson Brothers' finest early launches, with excellent speed and the smoothest ride on the river. She remained at Ina Island through a succession of owners over the next six decades, until in the early 1990s, when she was purchased by the present owner of Pullman Island, thus returning to her original home base on the river. In 2005, *Monitor*, still looking elegant and always attracting attention, will commence her one hundredth consecutive season in the Thousand Islands, within sight of where she was built.

At 38 feet overall, the open Launch Monitor
is larger than many mid-size cruisers.
Its length provides abundant carrying capacity,
a comfortable ride and an appearance
that always commands attention.

The terrace on Pullman Island affords a good look at the size of Monitor's cockpit.
Cruising in a large historic launch is a grand way to enjoy the splendor of the Thousand Islands.

At speed, the 1960 16-foot Cruisers Incorporated Seafarer is a smooth-riding craft with excellent visibility.

Birch Hill

A 16-Foot Outboard Runabout

Thompson, Lyman, Penn Yan and Cruisers Incorporated all built attractive, rugged little runabouts that operated very effectively with outboard motors. These modestly priced boats possessed appealing attributes that made them popular with boaters. One of the most appreciated attributes of these small outboard runabouts is their responsive steering. In other words, the boat goes where you expect it to go, and most experienced boaters understand the value of a boat that responds properly to what its

helmsman expects; however, nearly every single-engine inboard possesses steering characteristics that often defy the expectations of a driver who is unfamiliar with its steering quirks.

Birch Hill is the personal boat of the lady of the family, who claims "it's a joy to operate." She says that she simply wanted a boat that, in her own words, "goes where I point it." What more could a boater ask for! *Birch Hill* does just that, and that's why she's so popular among the boaters in the family. In addition to *Birch Hill's*

Birch Hill *safely nestled in her cozy boathouse on Cherry Island.*

The large mahogany-framed windshield and the attractive mahogany deck give Birch Hill *a very distinguished appearance.*

positive steering qualities, she is very soft-riding, planes quickly and has substantial speed with her 4-cylinder Johnson Seahorse engine, rated at 75 horsepower. In her early years she pulled water-skiers around a lot of islands on the river.

Birch Hill has never required restoration. She has been maintained well and still has all of the wood she possessed when she left the factory in Wisconsin in 1960. She won her class in the Alexandria Bay Boat Show and also won the coveted Renaissance Cup for her role in the culture of the river.

Birch Hill takes the shortcut to the main shipping channel of the St. Lawrence Seaway by passing under the Cherry Island footbridge.

The 23-foot runabout Our Ma *is a one-off Fitzgerald & Lee design with a Gar Wood windshield, hardware and instrument panel.*

Our Ma

Fitzgerald & Lee was a fine custom boatbuilding firm in Alexandria Bay, New York, from the mid-1920s until the beginning of the Second World War in 1941. They were also the authorized dealer for Gar Wood boats in the Thousand Islands region and very successful at both business activities. Many of their custom boats were equipped with Gar Wood hardware, windshields and dash instruments.

Our Ma is a wonderful 23-foot double-cockpit forward runabout with a Gar Wood folding windshield. She was built as a special custom design for Mrs. Mallory of Buck Island, who reportedly used the boat nearly every day for 35 years before deciding that it was time to sell her. In 1970 she was purchased by a classic boat enthusiast from Fishers Landing whose wife was the granddaughter of Alfred Lee, one of the original partners of the firm that built *Our Ma* in 1935.

The new owners were then, and still are, classic boat enthusiasts with several wonderful vintage boats in their collection, and *Our Ma* was thoughtfully restored to her original elegance. The current power is a 125-horsepower 6-cylinder Gray engine. Several times she has been an award-winning boat at regional classic boat shows. The owners say that their favorite award was the prestigious People's Choice Award received at the 1982 Clayton Antique Boat Show. *Our Ma* still resides at Fishers Landing on the river and has been operating in the Thousand Islands for more than 70 years.

For a runabout built in 1936, the rounded covering boards on Our Ma *present a very streamlined appearance.*

The builders of Our Ma *were also major Gar Wood dealers and often installed Gar Wood instruments and hardware on their custom-built boats.*

Our Ma *continues to be an outstanding example of Fitzgerald & Lee's craftsmanship and design skill.*

Baby Gar V *is a 33-foot reproduction of one of Gar Wood's most exciting designs of the 1920s.*

Baby Gar V

This boat is both unusual and superb in its presentation. It is, in fact, a reproduction of one of Gar Wood's personal racing runabouts, *Baby Gar V*, which he campaigned to promote his new line of Liberty-powered standardized 33-foot runabouts, which were known as Baby Gars. The original boat became famous, along with *Baby Gar IV*, when both boats challenged the crack New York Central express passenger train, the *Twentieth Century Limited*, to a race from Albany to New York City. The race was a great publicity stunt and resulted in fabulous media attention. Radio coverage of the race was broadcast from an airplane that followed the entire race. When Gar Wood won by 12 minutes, pictures of the event appeared on the front pages of major daily newspapers. Executives of the New York Central Railroad were furious and said they would never sanction a race with a boat. But it was too late and the race became an interesting piece of history. The results of this race immediately motivated Edward J. Noble, of the Life Saver Candy Company, to purchase his famous Baby Gar runabout, *Snail*, one of the legendary classic boats of the Thousand Islands.

The original hardware and fittings for Baby Gar V were faithfully reproduced to achieve as accurate a reproduction as possible.

The superb hull design of the original Baby Gar V set new standards for speed and performance for the entire boating industry.

119

Built using modern construction techniques, Baby Gar V *portrays the appearance and performance of the original 1925 racer.*

Of the seven original Baby Gars built specifically for racing, only the seventh survived. It one of the featured boats exhibited at the Antique Boat Museum. Numbers four and five were the most famous of the series, but they were broken up years ago. Number five was reproduced in 1995 using the standard Turcotte 33-foot runabout hull and making every effort to recreate a craft that is nearly a duplicate of the original. Powered by a 750-horsepower General Motors engine, the new *Baby Gar V* reproduces the speed and performance of the original raceboat. She is a frequent participant at classic boat shows throughout the Northeast, and her generous owner regularly offers rides to classic boat enthusiasts. *Baby Gar V* is a wonderful reproduction of a lost classic.

Kon Tiki

A 25-Foot Gar Wood Runabout

In 1932 Gar Wood felt that the introduction of a smaller-sized deluxe runabout might attract more sales activity than their 28- and 33-foot models. It was later that year that they introduced the 25-foot Deluxe runabout with its attractive folding-V windshield. The boat captured Gar Wood's classic lines superbly and was one of the best designs to emerge from the Great Depression, which had nearly crushed the pleasure-boat industry. At 25 feet it was a good-sized runabout, but even with all the deluxe features of the larger models, the price difference was not enough to lure the number of buyers anticipated. It remained in production through 1941, with sales increasing after the economy began to rebound. It is still considered one of Gar Wood's most appealing runabouts, and sought after by serious collectors.

Kon Tiki is one of these rare 25-foot runabouts. It was purchased by a publishing family who spent their summers on Wellesley Island in a marvelous section of the seaway known as the American Narrows. (The family owned the publishing firm that produced the famous book *Kon Tiki.*)

This view of Kon Tiki *shows all three cockpits and the attractive hull shape of the mid-1930s fast runabout.*

Kon Tiki shows how its 75-year-old hull can split a wave, to the delight of passengers on board the tour boat.

Kon Tiki *is one of the finest Gar Wood runabouts of the golden era of classic mahogany runabouts and still enjoys frequent use.*

At left: *The attractive foredeck of* Kon Tiki *is classic styling at its best.*

At right: Kon Tiki*'s soft leather roll-and-pleat front seat and the starboard windshield bracket with built-in navigation light.*

Commuters and Cruisers

5

At first, traveling from one island to another or from your island to the mainland in an open boat with your hair blowing was part of the sport of being in the islands. But as the social scene became more sophisticated and glamorous, the women of the islands prevailed upon their husbands to provide more suitable craft for commuting. The custom boat builders of the region had been outfitting their power launches with convertible tops to provide additional protection from wind and spray; however, this was not the complete answer to suit the fashionable dress at many of the gala events. A new craft was needed, and the island commuter emerged to fill this need. It was based largely on the designs developed by John Hacker in the mid-1920s for commuters, with town-car-type styling.

The Hacker designs featured 35- and 38-foot-high performance hulls capable of speeds in the range of 40 mph. The driver's cockpit was located forward of the smartly styled cabin enclosure, looking similar to the chauffer-driven automotive town car. The cabin was bright and comfortable, with convenient access from the large aft cockpit. The cabin interiors were styled for commuting, with chairs or settees rather than bunks. Usually the cabins were equipped with an enclosed lavatory and a suitable galley or bar. The primary purpose was to deliver the owner and passengers to their next location in style and comfort, without getting windblown or wet along the way. It was the ideal craft for the islands, and both Hutchinson and Fitzgerald & Lee turned out several extraordinary commuters that served the special needs of island families superbly.

Lizzy is a well-designed express cruiser
with a large open cockpit that is ideal for touring the islands with several passengers.

At about the same time, Gar Wood, Chris-Craft, Dodge and Hackercraft offered limousine enclosures for their larger runabouts. The cabin enclosures closely resembled the profile of automobiles of the same period. It would be safe to describe the cabin as a permanent top over the two forward cockpits of a triple-cockpit runabout. Rather than a front bench seat, the limousine version offered two bucket seats, permitting easier access inside. The cabin was entered through a sliding hatch in the aft section of the cabin roof and stepping down onto the bench seat in the cabin. The cabin entrance was reached by walking carefully over the engine hatch, which required a bit of agility. Although these limousines were popular, they provided considerably less room and comfort than the island commuters.

However, the Thousand Island boatbuilders also provided a successful alternative to larger and more expensive commuters It was called the sedan utility. This boat was essentially a sport-utility with an attractive cabin enclosure, featuring large glass windows on three sides with a full opening to the cockpit area. The cabin was a pleasant, airy enclosure that could be entered very easily. The cabin and the aft cockpit shared the same floor level, making access simple and convenient. The sport-utility sedan was smaller than the island commuter and normally operated by the owner rather than by a paid hand.

It was a practical, multi-purpose craft that became very popular among the islanders. In the early spring and in the late fall, when the temperatures were a bit chilly on the river, the sedan style provided

passengers with a snug enclosure. On the hottest days of mid-summer, the sedan's ventilating windshields allowed air to flow through, thus keeping the cabin comfortable while the enclosure protected passengers from the hot sun. Hutchinson also developed a sedan model that was powered with a V-drive transmission, permitting the engine to be located under the aft deck. This arrangement resulted in an unobstructed open cockpit and even easier cabin access.

The limousines, island commuters and sedans were all quite popular with Thousand Islands boaters from the time they were introduced in the 1920s through to the 1940s. From this time on, the use of attractive and simple folding canvas tops on sport boats increased to the point that they are now almost considered standard equipment.

Cruising slowly through the deep-water passages in and around the Thousand Islands is a spectacular treat that never loses its thrill. Delightfully close glimpses of the islands are often possible with the abundant water depth at their edges. The massive granite formations that rise sharply from the river bottom allow boaters the opportunity to study some of the Earth's oldest exposed rock.

As interest in the Thousand Islands spread among wealthy sportsmen, they responded to the natural beauty by constructing remarkable summer homes. Perhaps their island homes were a tribute to the river's magnificence or simply a lavish display of their personal wealth. Whatever the reason, cruising slowly through the island passages provides boaters and their guests with a wonderful display of architectural creativity that adds to the pleasure of each voyage.

In addition to scenic vistas, the Thousand Islands offer a multitude of wonderful destinations with harbors and excellent accommodations for overnight docking. Kingston, Gananoque, Rockport and Brockville on the Canadian side of the river offer superb harbors for cruisers, with hotels, restaurants, shops and attractions near the docks. On the American side of the river, Cape Vincent, Clayton, Alexandria Bay and Morristown offer excellent dockage and a wide range of attractive accommodations. Traveling a bit farther, Ottawa, Ogdensburg and Montreal provide an even wider range of activities. The abundance of wonderful destinations through relatively sheltered waterways makes this region a paradise for cruising.

Yachtsmen always enjoy cruising more when there is an interesting destination included. It may be a visit to the famous Antique Boat Museum in Clayton or the island castles of Singer and Boldt or to one of the many fine restaurants along the river. There are also superb state and national parks for swimming, hiking or overnight stays. The Thousand Islands region provides so many interesting locations for boaters that it would take several seasons of cruising to experience all that is offered.

The region has a well-deserved reputation for providing some of North America's most interesting boat tours and dinner cruises. There is so much to observe and learn that many visitors return year after year. The islands themselves also function as effective barriers to the build-up of heavy seas so common on the Great Lakes, allowing smooth, pleasant cruising most of the time.

This 33-foot Futura express set a new standard for Chris-Craft styling in the mid-1950s that continued until the end of wood construction in 1972.

The 1931 35-foot Hutchinson commuter A.C.S. moves slowly past her home port at Estrellita Island.

A.C.S.

A 1931 35-FOOT HUTCHINSON COMMUTER

The island commuter is a very special boat, designed to provide safe, comfortable transportation for a modest number of passengers to the mainland or from one island to the next. The substantial hull resembles the large displacement utility style, with a round bottom and full beam to provide a pleasant ride. The open chauffeur's station is forward and separate from the passenger cabin, with the cabin enclosure located amidships, easily accessible from the large, open cockpit. The commuter cabin has windows all around to provide passengers with an excellent opportunity to observe all that they pass by. The marine engine is normally located in an attractive mahogany enclosure in the cockpit. A chauffer was expected to operate the commuter for islanders and their guests upon request, providing swift, convenient transportation in grand style.

The island commuters are a wonderful throwback to a bygone era and still provide an elegant way to travel in a wide range of conditions. They are wonderfully snug in the early spring and late fall when the air is crisp and the river is still beautiful. A.C.S. continues to provide her owners with this enjoyable style of river transportation. There was a time when a large number of islanders possessed an enclosed commuter, and the tradition of using the owner's initials as the boat's name served a useful purpose to help guests identify the correct boat at a busy dock.

Even large commuters like A.C.S. are capable of high-speed performance when necessary.

The interior of the island commuter A.C.S. is paneled in mahogany, and offers a snug, comfortable cabin protected from severe weather.

Looking forward from the aft cockpit in A.C.S. towards the secure cabin enclosure.

The chauffeur's compartment is usually open but has a convertible top when needed.

The island commuter A.C.S. quietly waits for her passengers at home on Estrellita Island.

Hutchinson Boat Works and Fitzgerald & Lee in Alexandria Bay built many of the commuters. Although the general appearance of the commuters was similar, each was customized to fit the individual requirements of its owner. Many were equipped with a small bar for refreshments, a lavatory, a lounge and comfortable wicker chairs. The driver's station was generally left open, with a simple canvas top that could be used during rainy weather.

This commuter was originally built for Julia DuPont Tallman of Tar Baby Island and Wilmington, Delaware. She owned the boat for 30 years before selling. The new owner purchased the boat from her 44 years ago and still has it. At the time of purchase the boat was named with the owner's initials, *J.H.T.*, and the name so pleased the new owner that she decided to use her initials to rename the commuter *A.C.S.*

North Star *is a fine example of Chris-Craft's outstanding cruiser design in the late 1930s.*

North Star

A 1939 Chris-Craft Double-Cabin Enclosed-Bridge Cruiser Commuter

Mercer's Shipyard in Clayton was one of Chris-Craft's highest-volume dealers for several years and ranked as high as number two in total annual sales for the giant boat builder. Chris-Craft built their reputation on flashy varnished runabouts, but their real contribution was in designing and building attractive, comfortable cruisers. One style they really mastered was the Double-Cabin Enclosed-Bridge (DCEB) model. It was Chris-Craft more than any other builder that made this style popular and absolutely beautiful to observe. The 1939 36-footer *North Star* is a fine example of this style — beautifully proportioned and superbly designed for a cruiser of modest overall length.

The 36-foot DCEB model was the featured display model for Chris-Craft at the 1939 National Motor Boat Show and was an ideal model for cruising in the Thousand Islands. Mercer's was impressed and placed an order for one that would eventually be named *North Star*. She was sold immediately, and over the next several seasons would spend a great deal of time cruising Lake Ontario, the Finger Lakes and the Thousand Islands with each of her first five owners. She was retired in 1992 for repairs that were started but never completed. For three years she waited to be discovered. In 1995 she was sold, as is, to her present owner, who could visualize her classic beauty despite her undignified appearance. The boat was still quite original, and it would take the couple nearly ten years to complete all of the work required.

Today *North Star* is one of the most attractive vintage cruisers in the Thousand Islands. She is still quietly cruising through the islands with her single original Chris-Craft Model-M reduction-drive engine. She has a very comfortable interior, with a large deckhouse, a double stateroom aft, and galley and dinette forward. This is an excellent layout for extended cruising, entertaining or simply enjoying all that the islands have to offer.

The double-cabin enclosed-bridge-style cruiser
was a favorite design for Chris-Craft and by 1939 was nearing perfection.

Lady Ashley

A 25-FOOT SHEPHERD EXPRESS CRUISER

Shepherd was a major Canadian builder of fine boats. They were best known for their innovative sport boats, which established new design trends in the years after the Second World War. Their V-Drive sport boats successfully crossed the line between runabouts and utilities and created a style that still challenges boat-show judges to put them in the correct category.

Following Chris-Craft's approach of offering a complete line of boats, Shepherd expanded into the cruiser market in the late '50s to increase their market share. By 1965 they offered a full line of models from 19-foot runabouts to 46-foot motor yachts.

Lady Ashley is the 1963 express cruiser that Shepherd offered as a modest craft to introduce a family to the benefits of cruising. This model offered a generous cockpit and a delightful cabin that could sleep four comfortably, with a dinette, full galley and an enclosed head. Equipped with a single engine, this small cruiser is remarkably fuel efficient and as easy to maneuver as a sport-utility. *Lady Ashley's* home port is Kingston, Ontario, and she is one of the most active classics in the Thousand Islands, traveling to Montreal, Peterborough and Ottawa, as well as on the Trent River. She also makes trips to several U.S ports, and is a frequent participant in antique and classic boat shows.

Lady Ashley is an attractive Shepherd cruiser that is small enough to fit inside this boathouse, which is important in keeping it looking good.

Lady Ashley has the advantage of shallow draft, allowing it to travel into quiet bays.

Friendship *is one of Chris-Craft's most popular designs of the early post–Second World War era.*

Friendship

A 1950 30-Foot Chris-Craft Express Cruiser

Shortly after the conclusion of the Second World War, the market for small, fast express cruisers boomed along with the post-war economy. Chris-Craft had developed effective techniques for restyling their boats into new models without making wholesale changes to their proven hulls. Their ability to introduce changes each year without having to create an entirely new boat was one of their most valuable skills. As a result they could present a new series of models every year with a minimum of lost production time.

To introduce their new 30-foot express cruiser quickly, Chris-Craft utilized their stock 30-foot cruiser hull that had been in production for several years. It was an ideal hull and was easily transformed into a very attractive express cruiser. The new express model received a great reception among potential buyers and became one of Chris-Craft's best sellers for years, with only slight model-year changes. *Friendship* is an excellent example of this model and is perfectly suited to cruising on the river. She is equipped with a pair of 130-horsepower 6-cylinder Chris-Craft engines that provide excellent speed when required. Her interior offers the convenience of a comfortable dinette, a large galley, forward V-berths and an enclosed head. Her spacious cockpit is one of her most important attributes, providing a pleasant area for a small crowd while cruising.

Friendship's traditional Chris-Craft instrument cluster and nautical wheel is neat and completely original.

When this plate is displayed, you can bet the owners and their boat are a perfect fit.

Canvas spray shields were introduced by Chris-Craft at the 1940 National Motorboat Show and became one of their regular trademarks for more than a decade.

With its convertible top removed, Friendship *takes on the much sportier look of the open express cruiser.*

The current owners have added a well-designed extension to the standard convertible top. This feature allows the entire cockpit to be fully enclosed when cruising in rainy weather, as well as providing some welcome shade from the sun on hot summer days.

Friendship was originally purchased through Mercer's Shipyard in Clayton in 1950. Chris-Craft cruisers were in high demand, and choice models were at a premium, with many buyers feeling fortunate if they could find the one that they desired. The current owners of *Friendship* had many years of experience as marina operators and were very knowledgeable boaters. They acquired *Friendship* in 1988 and began a systematic ten-year approach to make all the improvements necessary for the boat to be attractive and reliable. Their plan involved using the boat during the boating season and doing the enhancements in the non-boating season, and they never lost one summer of cruising on the river while the attractive improvements continued each year. Today, *Friendship* is a beautiful example of one of Chris-Craft's most popular small cruisers and frequently receives awards at classic boat shows on both sides of the border.

The extended convertible top increases the use of the large cockpit on rainy days as well as on those days when the sun is too strong.

Rulette VIII docked alongside her boathouse on Round Island. This vintage fiberglass express cruiser has the lines of her wooden predecessors.

Rulette VIII

A 1969 31-Foot Bertram Express Cruiser

It may surprise some readers that a Bertram fiberglass cruiser is included in a book of classic boats. However, *Rulette VIII* was purchased at the Bertram factory in 1969 and spent her entire life with the same family in the Thousand Islands. Now over 35 years old, she has been recognized by Boating U.S. as the one of the best powerboats ever built. The innovative hull, designed by naval architect Ray Hunt in 1960 for Dick Bertram, was created to win the exciting offshore race from Miami to Nassau. It was based on a hull that Bertram had made history with in the 1960 race in a boat named *Moppie*. Challenged by 8-foot seas and 30-knot winds, *Moppie* blew the competition away and won the race in record time, two and a half hours ahead of the second-place boat.

The Bertram 31 represented a sharp change in hull design, featuring a deep-vee configuration with lifting strakes all the way to the transom. Bertram's spectacular victory effectively changed hull design for performance-oriented mono-hulled boats. It handles heavy seas safely with little discomfort and is easy to control in following seas or headwinds.

Rulette VIII (the combined names RUth and FolLETTE) has a generous open cockpit that accounts for nearly half of the boat. Its interior has an enclosed head, a dinette that converts to a double berth, a compact galley and V-berths forward. Her elevated control station provides the helmsman with outstanding visibility. She is an outstanding cruising boat that is comfortable and can provide marvelous speed with her twin 340-horsepower Marine Power engines. After nearly 40 consecutive seasons serving her Round Island owners, *Rulette VIII* is both a fiberglass classic and a Thousand Islands classic.

The vintage Bertram express cruiser's cabin is delightfully bright with the extensive use of large windows all around.

The Futura is a rugged cruiser that offers excellent speed and the positive wave-handling qualities of a larger vessel.

Lizzy

The decade following the Second World War introduced new styles to the boatbuilding industry. Pleasure boating was becoming the new pastime for thousands of North Americans. The giant boatbuilding corporation Chris-Craft continued in their pre-war position as the world's leader in total production as well as influencing the popular styling trends. By the mid-1950s their special treatment of the stem on their new models was so extreme that boaters often referred to it as the "bull nose bow." Chris-Craft sensed it was time for a styling change.

In 1956 Chris-Craft developed a totally new 33-foot express cruiser with a classic clipper bow and a raised sheer that flows gracefully to the large, open cockpit. This marvelous new boat was a glimpse of the future styling for Chris-Craft. Appropriately, they named their new model the Futura, and a whole new trend was underway. The trend was so popular that it influenced the treatment of all wood Chris-Crafts through the '60s, until wood construction ended forever in 1972.

Lizzy is the twelfth Futura model built in the series of 118 over four years of production. Powered by twin Chris-Craft V-8 engines, *Lizzy* has a top speed close to 30 mph. However, the preferred mode of operation to provide guests with a more enjoyable cruise is closer to 8 mph. Her spacious teak cockpit offers a congenial location in which to enjoy a pleasant tour of the islands. *Lizzy's* home port is Cherry Island, where she shares her boathouse with *Belacqua*, the family's 26-foot Lyman.

The massive bow fairleader is both stylish and well suited for guiding the anchor line.

Wide walk-around decks with lifelines provide important security and peace of mind.

Dual horns at the base of the mast are a standard Chris-Craft feature.

The Cub

A 1917 First World War Harbor Launch

he Cub is one of the better-known workboats of the Thousand Islands. She was built at the Consolidated Shipyard at City Island, New York, in 1917, along with several other boats, in fulfillment of a military contract during the First World War. The contract called for several motorized ship's launches for harbor duty for the United States Navy. Built to the substantial specifications required for the navy, the craft is exceedingly robust and has endured decades of heavy work. A year after the armistice was signed, she was declared government surplus and sold at a fraction of her cost at public auction. When she arrived in the Thousand Islands, she was utilized as a multi-purpose workboat for the Thomas Mitchell Lumber Yard on Wellesley Island.

Years later, in 1976, a barge loaded with crude oil went off course in the American Narrows of the St. Lawrence Seaway. The barge's hull ruptured, spilling its thick crude petroleum into the pristine river just above the village of Alexandria Bay. The spill was a major environmental disaster, and every available workboat on the river was required to help contain it. *The Cub* was called into government service once more to aid the heroic efforts to save the river and protect the wildlife.

Every day for four months *The Cub* was on duty with equipment that provided pressurized hot water to clean the oil slick from everything it touched. By late fall her work was completed and she took on a new role as a utility boat for Cherry Island. After several years of hard labor, *The Cub* was sold to the owner of Pullman Island and re-powered with a new diesel engine. She was painted, spruced up and fitted out with a large American flag. *The Cub* continues to serve her owners well and has finally been elevated to the role of well-maintained multi-purpose boat, even showing up at vintage boat shows in a special workboat category.

*The Cub has worked hard throughout her life on the St. Lawrence River
and proudly wears the First World War U.S. Navy standard-issue gray paint scheme.*

145

The Museum's In-Water Fleet

T here are many reasons why the Antique Boat Museum in Clayton, New York, is very special to those who enjoy the history of pleasure boating in North America. One of the features that helps to define this museum's special character is the opportunity provided visitors to actually experience riding in authentic vintage boats on the St. Lawrence River. The museum has carefully designated specific boats for these trips, which range in size from 28-foot triple-cockpit runabouts to 42-foot high-speed commuters.

While viewing the museum's boats in the static exhibits is an excellent way to study their design details and construction, the opportunity to see them perform is a special treat. The activity is also an unusual use of a museum artifact and requires a carefully organized program. Each in-water boat is inspected and certified by the United States Coast Guard and operated only by certified captains under carefully controlled circumstances. The boats are maintained very diligently, and the captains submit daily reports on the operation and condition of each boat that is operated. All boats are also subject to regular inspections.

The boats are part of the museum's permanent collection and must meet all current United States Coast Guard regulations and be ready for inspections at all times. The boats that comprise the in-water fleet may rotate from one season to the next depending upon the need for repairs, refinishing or changes in the program's goals. The following six boats were operational in the 2004 season.

Three great classics, Zipper, Gadfly and Teal, are all components of the Antique Boat Museum's 2004 in-water fleet, providing a delightful way to see the Thousand Islands.

Ariel, a 1885 steam launch built by Charles Seabury, is one of the oldest active powerboats in the Thousand Islands.

Ariel

A 25-FOOT STEAM-POWERED LAUNCH

Charles Seabury's company built *Ariel* in 1885 as a steam-powered launch. *Ariel's* original steam engine was replaced several years ago with a conventional gasoline-powered engine when steam power became too cumbersome compared to the convenience of the gasoline marine engine. Currently, however, she is once again powered with a double-action single-cylinder steam engine, displacing 51.5 cubic inches and producing approximately 5 horsepower. The steam engine came from the Antique Boat Museum's collection of engines and dates back to around 1875. The conversion to gas power was a common change for older steam-powered launches

that still had a useful future with an alternate form of power.

Steam power required massive engines that needed to be placed in the middle of the craft, taking space that could be better devoted to passengers or freight. It was also a time when alternative power was being developed that would be better suited for small craft. The early gasoline engines were relatively inexpensive to purchase, more efficient than steam and could be located out of the way. *Ariel* has been carefully restored and is in perfect running condition, providing the museum and visitors with an authentic steam-powered launch to enjoy and study.

Beautifully restored, Idyll Oaks *led the boat parade at the very first antique boat show in North America, held 40 years ago in the Thousand Islands.*

Idyll Oaks

A 1924 26-FOOT HUTCHINSON LAUNCH

In 1964 *Idyll Oaks* was "discovered" in the back corner of a marina storage building in Clayton. She was 40 years old when her owner abandoned her for the amount of her unpaid storage and repair bill. When a prospective buyer and his wife were walking through the marina, the boat was barely visible in the dimly lit building. But the boat's long, attractive deck, spacious cockpit and the contours of her hull impressed the couple. The marina owner was happy to sell the boat for the amount owed, and the couple was even happier to take on ownership of the old boat. Their cottage on the river was named *Idyll Oaks*, and they decided it would be appropriate give the old launch the same name.

By the following summer *Idyll Oaks* had received a winter's worth of work to get her fully prepared for a long summer on the river. She looked so good that the new owners invited several friends with wooden boats to help organize a public boat show for older wooden boats. The Clayton Chamber of Commerce liked the idea, and the 1965 event became the world's first official antique boat show. The momentum from the event was so strong that it provided inspiration for the establishment of the Antique Boat Museum and for organizing other antique boat shows around the world.

Idyll Oaks enjoyed the company of new owners in the decades following the first antique boat show; however, her final private owner, Dan Morrow, felt that she was so important to the history of the Thousand Islands that she should be given to the Antique Boat Museum. The boat was such a significant gift that the museum arranged to have her fully restored to her original beauty.

In the summer of 2004, 40 years after *Idyll Oaks* was found and 80 years after she was constructed at the Hutchinson Boat Works, she returned to the event she had started, leading the parade of nearly a hundred antique boats during the 40th Annual Clayton Antique Boat Show.

Relatively new by museum standards, Teal *is an accurately reproduced 1938 triple-cockpit Gar Wood runabout built in 1988 by the Turcotte Brothers and well known throughout the Thousand Islands.*

Teal

A 1988 28-FOOT TURCOTTE GAR WOOD

For 17 years, *Teal* has been one of the most frequently observed boats each season, cruising and sometimes speeding in the Thousand Islands. But she is a not as old as her design would lead us to believe. She is a reproduction of a 1938 Gar Wood built under the scrupulous supervision of Tom and Larry Turcotte. The Turcotte brothers fell in love with Gar Wood boats as youngsters and in the 1980s made a decision to keep the Gar Wood tradition alive by building a new series of boats with modern techniques and modern power. *Teal* is a superb example of their skill and attention to detail.

Initially, a summer resident from Bluff Island, near Clayton, purchased *Teal* for his personal use. He was also an active trustee of the Antique Boat Museum, and soon envisioned a wonderful new role for *Teal* as a component of an in-water fleet of classic boats to extend the museum's activities throughout the Thousand Islands. *Teal* was donated to the museum and has been driven thousands of miles with special guests, attending classic boat shows, going on long-distance cruises and commuting to various island events. *Teal*'s physical condition is remarkable, considering the

constant use that she receives, and speaks well to the quality of her construction. The Turcotte brothers continue to provide service whenever *Teal* needs another coat of varnish or when the upholstery shows wear from years of constant use.

Currently powered by a new 454 V-8 Crusader, *Teal* is capable of thrilling speeds above 40 mph with a full complement of passengers in all three cockpits. She continues to be a favorite among museum visitors, who love her classic good looks and superb performance.

Although *Teal* is not really a 1938 vintage Gar Wood, there is no way to distinguish her modern construction technology from her outward appearance. In every way she appears to be a well-cared-for, 65-year-old boat similar to others in the museum's permanent collection. The benefit of her modern construction is her ability to gracefully endure the frequency with which she is used. The 28-foot triple-cockpit Gar Wood runabouts were the highest production models of any Gar Wood in the pre–Second World War period, from 1922 through 1941.

*Zipper is the flagship of the museum's in-water fleet, traveling to boat shows,
touring with guests and taking friends of the museum on special cruises.*

Zipper

A 42-Foot Staudacher/Purdy Commuting Cruiser

During the years just before the Great Depression, the Stroh family, famous for their brewery and fine beers, asked Ned Purdy to design a commuting cruiser for their boating activities. The design was prepared and approved. However, before construction could begin, the world economy was drawn into a full-scale depression. For four years the boatbuilding firms seemed to be hit extremely hard, and many did not survive. Purdy's Boat Yard was among those that were forced to close.

Years later the Stroh family looked again at the wonderful plans for the commuter and decided to build it just the way it had been designed three decades earlier. The well-established Michigan boatbuilder Staudacher was selected to build the commuter for the Strohs. Staudacher suggested that the hull should be built using a form of cold molding technology to build an exceptionally strong and attractive mahogany hull. The result was a spectacular craft that combined the classic styling of a vintage commuter with advanced construction technology.

After enjoying *Zipper* for several seasons, the Strohs chose to donate their commuter to the Antique Boat Museum, where she could remain in service by providing classic boating enthusiasts with the pleasure of riding in a fast, vintage-style commuter. *Zipper* has become the flagship of the museum's in-water fleet and is a wonderful symbol of class boating throughout the region. She is superbly maintained and is equipped to meet all of the rigorous safety criteria required by the United States Coast Guard for approved passenger service.

Powered by twin 454 Crusader engines, *Zipper* is a swift, soft-riding cruiser with runabout performance that is enjoyed by hundreds of guests each season. A special treat is to ride in the large forward cockpit, where the sound of the engines is hardly audible as the *Zipper* speeds smoothly towards her destination.

Zipper's magnificent tumblehome hull design can be appreciated from the stern view.

153

Miss Thousand Islands

The Antique Boat Museum offers visitors the thrills and pure joy of an old-fashioned speedboat ride in *Miss Thousand Islands*. Using a modern, vintage-style, triple-cockpit runabout with epoxy-enhanced mahogany construction and modern V-8 power, *Miss T.I.* (as she is often called) brings back fond memories of that first speedboat ride, with the spray forming huge wings of water. For many thrill riders it is the closest thing to flying, and the memory of that thrill is as vivid today as it was in childhood.

The Morgan/Hacker boat works (still called the Hacker Boat Company) on Lake George, New York, uses the superb designs of John Hacker with creative innovations to improve both comfort and performance. The boats appear in every way to be vintage models; however, there are subtle improvements that enhance the hull's excellent level-riding qualities and overall speed.

Miss T.I. is one of the most popular attractions at the museum, and was a gift from the builder, William Morgan, to be used as a special ride boat in recreating the heyday of speedboat thrill rides of the 1930s and 1940s. Accounts indicate that the original Hacker Boat Company contributed more innovations and improvements to the development of fast pleasure craft than any other boat-builder. Hacker was the first to recognize the potential of V-bottom construction and produced the first hydroplane to reach and exceed 50 mph and the first runabouts to exceed 50 mph and 60 mph.

Miss Thousand Islands provides exciting speedboat thrill rides for visitors to the museum all summer.

Gadfly

A 1931 33-Foot Hutchinson Sedan Cruiser

Sometimes they were called island commuters, but mostly they were referred to as sedans. They were a welcome treat for islanders for whom boats were the only way to connect to the mainland. The chauffer-driven sedan meant a comfortable, secure trip to another island or to the Canadian or American mainland.

From 1930 to 1939 Hutchinson Boat Works built a remarkable number of sedans, as they became the islanders' choice for comfortable river travel. The commuters ranged in length from 28 feet to 40 feet, and most of them had single-engine power in spite of their size. A few had the new Chrysler V-Drive transmissions, with the engine snugly located under the aft deck. The V-Drive arrangement provided the boats with the advantage of a larger, unobstructed cockpit area.

Gadfly is one of the popular 33-foot models, originally built for a family from Linden Cove along the American Narrows. Mexican mahogany was selected for her planking, and her cost was nearly $10,000 in 1931. Subsequent owners moved her to Michigan, where she was operated for several seasons. In the mid-1990s her owners contacted the director the Antique Boat Museum to return *Gadfly*

In the middle position between Zipper *and* Teal
is the elegant sedan Gadfly.

to her original home waters as part of the active in-water fleet. She was gladly accepted and adopted by a small group of museum friends, who take great pride in maintaining her in superb condition. Gadfly has become an extremely popular boat and travels to numerous events each season.

A view of one of the larger key-man restoration shops, with space to keep several boats inside in order to rotate work assignments.

Regional Restoration Shops

The building of boats as a robust industry in the Thousand Islands has quietly passed. There are a few individual craftsmen who still build one-off boats or build a few rowing skiffs for special customers. But in spite of the decline in boat-building, the Thousand Islands region still has an abundance of wooden boats that require seasonal refinishing as well as total restoration and rebuilding. As a result, skilled craftsmen in the Thousand Islands continue their trade by handling repairs and refinishing the boats that some of their fathers and grandfathers helped build years before. Progressively, this small core of independent boat refinishers has expanded their skills to become total restoration specialists.

Some restoration specialists work independently while others combine their talents as part of a comprehensive organization that provides the full range of restoration services. The regional tradition in which off-season fishing guides take on boat work during the winter season still continues to some extent. Some guides work at contemporary marina shops while others run their own one-man operations, where all the work takes place in an oversized garage or small building.

Some restoration shops have grown significantly in recent years to become full-service facilities with a staff of specialists. As interest in classic boats grows, it is becoming increasingly difficult to find well-preserved examples of specific models. As a result, the quest for a specific boat may turn up a derelict example that offers little more than the pattern to accurately create a reproduction. As the need for handling extensive restoration challenges grows, the full-service shop is increasingly being called upon to do more than to refinish or repair a vintage boat.

The full-service shop offers some advantages that may be vital to the successful completion to the project. Having a team of specialists can result in much greater efficiency by reducing the time consumed to solve difficult problems. Larger restoration shops are usually fully equipped with a wide range of equipment that can reduce labor costs. Normally, the full-service shop is also well stocked with the materials required to complete the task. Simply having a substantial inventory of quality marine hardwoods facilitates proper selection without waiting for special orders to be delivered.

In some full-service shops special facilities are available for a variety of repairs and reconstruction work. One of the newest facilities in the region was designed specifically for performing a wide range of restoration activities. Ease of access, separation of activities, lighting and temperature controls were all well planned. There is a separate shop for woodworking with a complete complement of modern power tools and ample room to work on several boats in the same well-illuminated area. The special finishing room is isolated from other work activities and equipped with temperature and humidity controls. The floor has large drains to facilitate frequent washdowns. In addition to the work areas, there is a significant amount of secure inside storage for boats scheduled for restoration.

Shops of this magnitude can handle everything from a seasonal coat of varnish to creating a duplicate boat. The skill level evident in some shops is close to what was common in custom boatbuilding shops in the Thousand Islands 75 years ago. Many of the traditional woodworking methods and tools of the trade were passed on from one generation to the next among river families.

Currently, many of the local fishing guides stay busy during the winter season refinishing and restoring wooden boats for summer residents. The Thousand Islands is still a location where there is an abundance of local knowledge to handle a wide range of restoration needs. Even more, there is a sense of pride in this region where the

finest boats were once produced that the talent required to restore boats properly is still available. From Cape Vincent to Canton there are dozens of skilled, knowledgeable craftsmen that restore boats properly and can reproduce a classic design entirely in their shop. Each type of shop offers its own special set of advantages, but in many cases the final selection for restoration of a precious old boat has more to do with intangibles and personalities than it does with the facilities.

One of the key-man restoration shops is located in the building that was the location of Fitzgerald & Lee 60 years ago. This facility has all the ambiance of a traditional boatbuilding shop and located at the water's edge, providing easy access for wood boats in active use that may require a quick repair. There is enough space for four or five boats inside the shop so that similar types of work activities can be rotated from one project to another.

This restoration shop has the advantage of a waterfront location to service vintage boats conveniently when a situation arises quickly.

Installing a new bottom is one of the most frequent restoration tasks requested and is a good place to begin.

The varnishing room in this full-service restoration shop has a dust-free, temperature-and-humidity-controlled finishing room that goes a long way in assuring a superior finish.

Carpentry and planking activities require well-designed facilities and need to be isolated from the finishing activities.

As a single-man restoration shop it's vital for the owner to maintain contact with various specialists in the area who can be engaged when there is a repair related to their special talent. As a result, the small shop can effectively use specialists with specific expertise to solve complex problems by contracting without having them on the weekly payroll. While this is often efficient, the downside is that the small shop can only make use of this special arrangement when specialists are available. Delays in availability can result in holdups that influence the timely completion of a major job.

Classic boat owners often feel more comfortable dealing directly with the individual who is doing the work on their boat. This direct contact is an advantage usually associated with the small restoration shop. When the relationship between the boat owner and the restorer is open and comfortable, important decisions can be made together. The boat owner may feel a greater sense of control by being involved in the cost decisions of each phase of the project. Having the opportunity to build a comfortable relationship with the restorer is often vital to the project. The amount of work that a complex restoration project might need can sometimes be shocking.

Whichever type of restoration shop is required, the style of boat and the shop's specialization should match. Examples of previous work should be examined in order to make qualified choices. The Thousand Islands region continues to provide classic boaters with many excellent choices for quality work performed by craftsmen with a thorough knowledge of and respect for boatbuilding traditions.

Acknowledgments

We would like to thank: Bobby Bannister, Duane Chalk, Dick Calabrese, Richard Cardamone, Jim Cumming, Ed Deming, Bud Garlock, Kitt and Dan Goodwin, Follett Hodgkins, Jim Holden, Rebecca Hopfinger, Morris Huck, Richard Jury, Ernie King, Bill Knorr, Mike Mahoney, Teddy McNally, Peter McShane, Chuck Molson, Alex Mosher, Anne Potter, Sam Rivoli, Charles Snelling, Robert Tague, Michael Touchette, Addison (Trey) Vars and Howard Williams for allowing us the opportunity to photograph their beautiful boats, thanks to the staff of the Antique Boat Museum for bringing all their boats out on the river at the same time to be photographed. A special thanks to Gary DeYoung who always believes in our projects.

Bibliography

Fostle, D. W. "The Boatbuilders of Alexandria Bay." *Wooden Boat,*(September/October 1982): 66–72 and (November/December, 1982): 58–64.

Keats, John. *The Skiff and the River*. Nantucket, MA: The Herrick Collection, 1988.

Koroknay, Tom. *Lyman Boats: Legend of the Lakes*, Lexington, OH, 2004.

Mollica, Anthony S. *The American Wooden Runabout*. St. Paul, MN: MBI Publishing, 2002.

Mollica, Anthony S. *Castles & Cottages*. Erin, ON: Boston Mills Press, 2004.

Mollica, Anthony S. *Gar Wood Boats: Classics of a Golden Era*. St. Paul, MN: MBI Publishing, 1999.

Ross, Don. *Discovering the Thousand Islands*. Brockville, ON:Henderson Printing, 2003.

"The St. Lawrence Skiff." *The Thousand Islands Sun*. May 19, 2004.Wilkinson, Bonnie. "Hutchinson Boat Works." *The Gazette Annual (1999)*: 10–20.

Wren, Sally-Ann and Patrick. "The Boatbuilders of Muskoka." *The Gazette Annual* (2000):14–23.

Index of Featured Boats